W9-CKH-530

Diapers & Dishes or Pinstripes & Pumps

Christian Women in a Changing World

Gigi Graham Tchividjian

THOMAS NELSON PUBLISHERS
Nashville • Camden • Kansas City

Published in Nashville, Tennessee, by Thomas Nelson, Inc., and distributed in Canada by Lawson Falle, Ltd., Cambridge, Ontario.

Printed in the United States of America.

Library of Congress Cataloging-in-Publication Data

Tchividjian, Gigi.
Diapers and dishes or pinstripes and pumps?

Bibliography: p.
1. Women—Religious life. 2. Woman—Conduct of life. 3. Tchividjian, Gigi. I. Title.
BV4527.T44 1987 248.8′43 86–33307
ISBN 0-8407-5530-9

1 2 3 4 5 6 7 8 — 92 91 90 89 88 87

Sarah, this book is dedicated to you:
a beautiful example of a consistent Christian woman
in a changing world.

With Sincere Gratitude

To Stephan whose encouragement got me started and kept me going.

To Stephan-Nelson, Lisa, Berdjette, Basyle, Tullian, Aram, Jerushah, and Antony, who unselfishly gave their mother time to write.

To Sarah, who faithfully and cheerfully worked long, hard hours picking up the many responsibilities I had to relinquish while writing. You know that I simply could not have done it without you.

To Janet Thoma, my editor and friend, who placed me on my writing toes and kept me there.

To all the staff at Thomas Nelson who made this book a reality.

I simply and humbly say, "Thank you."

Contents

1 Questions, Questions,

I Have So Many Questions

It was a crisp October day at my parents' home in the mountains of North Carolina, which is snuggled three-fourths of the way up Little Piney, a cove with two "hog back" ridges extending down on either side like long protective arms.

Nothing quite compares to the beauty of an autumn day in the Blue Ridge Mountains. People travel many miles each year to enjoy the splendor of these mountains which are ablaze with varying degrees of reds and golds set against a clear, brilliant blue sky.

Although the air this particular day was fresh and bright, a breeze was blowing strongly enough to disturb the party decorations I had just finished placing outside on the front porch with the help of my two-and-a-half-year-old, Stephan-Nelson. We were in a hurry to get ready for his little sister Berdjette's first birthday party so we quickly rearranged the brightly colored cups and plates on the antique table, placing little chairs neatly in front of each place.

When we finished, I glanced once again across the Black Mountain Valley to the mountain ridge beyond. *No wonder they're called the Blue Ridge Mountains,* I thought. On certain days, like today, they were almost as blue as the sky, making it difficult to tell where the mountains ended and the sky began. But, depending on the time of day, or how the shadows fell, the ridges and coves directly across the valley often took on a deep dark color which gave the little town of Black Mountain its name.

Once again, a gust of wind interrupted my thoughts, picked up the cups and napkins, and scattered them all over the yard. Stephan-Nelson by now was becoming increasingly agitated and impatient with this unseen enemy that kept threatening to destroy his sister's birthday party. Suddenly, he darted out into the middle of the yard and lifted his little hand defiantly to the sky and shouted, "Stop!"

Of course, the wind didn't stop.

Often I feel just as Stephan-Nelson did that day. The winds of change seem to blow so frequently and so strongly that they destroy the order of my life until I want to throw up my arms and cry, "Stop!" Anne Morrow Lindbergh felt much the same way when she said in 1940, "The wave of the future is coming and there is no fighting it."

The role of women in the last fifty years has undergone so many changes that many of us feel as if we are caught in the middle of a storm rather then just a gust of wind. Women in recent years have experienced much of the future shock that Alvin Toffler talked about in his book *Future Shock*. We were raised with one set of values and now try to function in a society that has another set of standards. The new ad campaign for South Florida is "The rules are different here." Many of us could say this about our present-day society.

SIGNS OF CHANGE

Not long ago, a friend told me about her mother's experience when their family first moved to Florida some forty years ago. Her mother went out to purchase a refrigerator and was told by the salesman, in no uncertain terms, that she would need her husband's permission first.

Compare this experience to what I saw a couple of years ago when I went to purchase some paint in a paint and decorating store in the same state. As I was paying the bill, I noticed a sign behind the desk that read, "Husbands must have their wives' written consent before we will custom mix paint colors." Things certainly have changed.

Elizabeth Stanton and Susan B. Anthony would be thrilled by many of the changes that have taken place in the sixty-five years since woman's suffrage, but did they foresee all the results? They, too, would be concerned by many of the negative changes we have to contend with. One out of every two marriages fails. Every twenty-seven seconds a couple in this country gets divorced.[1] Twenty percent of all births are by single mothers. One-fifth of all homes are headed by a single mother. Nine million children are in need of child care because their mothers work. One out of every three children will watch their parents separate and will become victims of divorce, totaling more than twelve million American children under the age of eighteen whose parents are divorced. The escalating divorce rate has led to vicious custody battles and child snatching, and more than 1.5 million abortions will be performed this year, and 18 percent of those babies who *are* born, will be born to unwed mothers.[2]

According to a new study, college-educated women who are still single at the age of thirty-five have only a five percent chance of ever getting married.[3] These woman have discovered that when they reach thirty-five, they are no longer equal. Their biological clocks are running out. Many of these women suffer from terrible loneliness. Many have resorted to having babies out of wedlock just to have someone "who needs me" as one single mother put it.

As more and more marriages break up, leaving women to fend for themselves, and more women realize they may never marry, women are being pushed into the work force which often places them in situations where they have to be assertive and even aggressive. They are forced to face difficult situations at work with the boss and the competition as well as at home with the bill collector, the bank, and the school principal.

Eating disorders are surfacing, according to *American Health*, not only because young women are under great pressure to be thin—which to many is synonymous with beauty—but because they are also pressured to be "strong" in other ways, too. "For the first time in memory," this magazine says, "young women are expected to grow up more like their fathers than like their mothers. With rapid social change, girls are being asked in adolescence to become suddenly like boys: both break the ties and become independent high achievers. . . . They must succeed on male terms, landing important jobs and becoming self-reliant."[4] This article goes on to say how many of these young women rage against their mothers for not providing an example. However, aggressiveness, self-reliance and independence were not expected of our grandmothers nor of our mothers.

Elisabeth Elliot observes that "many women in the Woman's Movement, while telling themselves that they have come a long way have actually retreated to a partial humanity, one that refuses to acknowledge the *significance* of the sexual differentiation. And the woman who ignores this, ironically misses the very thing she has set out to find. By refusing to fulfill the whole vocation of womanhood she settles for a caricature, a pseudo-personhood."[5]

I would dare to say that most of us appreciate many of the positive changes in our society—new opportunities, the many options and privileges now open to women—but we feel very uncomfortable with and confused by the negative changes that have taken place. But, whatever feelings you or I may have, we are not going to be able to stand up and throw our arms in the air and stop the process of change.

If we can't stop these changes, how can we as Christian women live in and adapt to today's changing world? What about the changing values, "the new rules"? Does adapting necessarily mean accepting and then conforming to them? I have a friend who says that many Christians tend to stay as close to the line of compromise as they possibly can, to the point of straddling or even crossing the line.

How do we instill biblical convictions and lasting moral values in our children? Especially when they see all around them Christians, even Christian leaders, who are compromising and rationalizing the moral values and absolutes that are clearly set forth in Scripture? Divorce seems to have become quite fashionable even among Christians.

A few years ago, a well-known Christian TV personality was invited to address a civic breakfast near our home in Fort Lauderdale, Florida. He arrived with a beautiful dark-haired woman. When the honored guests were introduced, the young woman was identified as his wife. The silence was suddenly broken by an audible gasp of surprise from the audience. His first wife, whom most of those present had taken for granted was still his wife, had been a blond.

Not long after that incident, I was appalled to hear a prominent Christian leader take more than an hour to explain to her radio audience why she had decided to leave her husband after thirty years of marriage and marry another prominent man in Christian work.

I have begun to feel like my little son Aram, who was once driving to Miami with his father and me when we passed several traffic accidents. When we passed the third one, he said, "Mama, there are almost as many accidents here as there are divorces."

What do we teach our children about marriage and family? Do we tell them that marriage is a beautiful, binding covenant between God and two people that lasts "until death do us part"? Or do we compromise and discourage all that we hold sacred? With the statistics blaring at us, what do we tell our daughters? Do we encourage them to marry and have a family or do we push them toward a career, self-reliance, and independence?

Should culture or circumstances alter our convictions or our commitment?

Do we personally have convictions to live by?

In *The Feminine Mystique*, Betty Friedan wrote that the core of women's problems today is a problem of identity. Is it true, as many say, that to find our own identity and be fulfilled we must seek opportunities outside the home? How do Christian women in today's twentieth-century world become and do all that is expected of them?

We are told at every turn that we can do anything and that we should be doing more. Every time we pick up a magazine, Christian ones included, we are told about yet another pursuit we should follow—diet and exercise plans, investment opportunities, beauty regimens, get-rich-quick schemes. How can we find the time to accommodate all of these helpful suggestions when they would have to be added to our already full and overextended calendars?

Feminists tell us that we are invincible. That we can do anything, be anything, and play several different roles at once. They encourage us to stretch ourselves almost to the snapping point. My husband, Stephan, is a psychologist, and his office is filled with women who are suffering from frustration, anxiety, and burnout. For some, he says, it's almost too late. They have tried for too long to fit the Superwoman image and now they're at the breaking point. How do they find the physical, emotional, and spiritual rest they so desperately need?

Many of us were also brought up with biblical principles like the teaching in First Peter that says a gentle, quiet spirit in a woman is of great price in the sight of God. What does this mean for us today?

How should a Christian woman live in the world today? What is a normal Christian woman?

This past summer, Stephan and I went away for two weeks and left the children at home in Florida. When we returned, we were met by seven eager faces all talking at once. They wanted to know all the exciting details of our trip. And we did have a few. We had spent five wonderful days in Israel and a glorious week in Switzerland. We had also experienced several "firsts." We enjoyed our first ride in a helicopter which flew us from Geneva, Switzerland, skirting the lovely lake, past sleepy villages and large cities till we reached the mountain pass. Then we slowly ascended till we reached the top and there stretching out before us was a panoramic view of the Swiss Alps. It was a once-in-a-lifetime experience and the children were hungry to hear about it.

Another evening I was working in my hotel room in Switzerland, when Stephan arrived and said, "Honey, get ready because we're going up in a hot-air balloon at six o'clock." I couldn't believe my ears. Another first for sure. But what a glorious experience! Soaring high above the valleys and farms surrounded by breathtaking beauty, silence, and towering mountain peaks. Little three-year-old Antony was beside himself with excitement as we told our story. He wanted to know all about the big airplanes that had taken mama and daddy to these wonderful places. When Antony got his turn (by interrupting his brothers and sisters repeatedly) to ask questions, he said, "Mama, you went on an airplane?"

"Yes," I replied.

"A big, big, big airplane?" he asked, throwing his little arms as wide as he could.

"Yes, dear, a very big one," I said as I looked into his bright, shining eyes.

"Mama, did you go in a helicopter, too?"

"Yes," I quickly replied before he popped the next question.

"Also a hot-air balloon?" he asked even more excitedly.

"Yes, darling," I answered again.

This proved too much for him. He could not contain his enthusiasm and his words began to tumble all over one another. He became frustrated and exasperated, and making a defeated gesture with his small hands, he sighed heavily and said, "Mama, I have so many questions!"

Antony dear, I, too, have so many questions. And to all of these questions that I have raised in this first chapter, I have to answer, "I don't know. I am still searching my heart and the Word of God for the answers."

The purpose of this book is to allow us to explore some of these thoughts and questions together. It will not cover all of our questions nor attempt to answer them all. I cannot make decisions for you, but I can help you discover through the Scriptures the freedom God gives us to make individual choices. I trust this book will cause you to think and to search God's Word for a better understanding of the way He would have us live as Christian women in a changing world.

2 Are You Liberated?

Each time I stand in line at the checkout counter of the grocery store, I am amused by the titles of the articles shown on the covers of women's magazines. "How to Be Married and Free" . . . which assumes that marriage is bondage. "Liberated Looks, Lifestyle, and Love" . . . which encourages women to be "liberated" in every area of their lives. Others read, "Fragrance Freedom," "Hair Liberation," and "America's New Independent Woman."

The word *free* seems to have become the panacea of today, almost a sacred word to the women's movement. Just as the magazine article titles indicate, this word conveys various images to our minds. Stop for a moment and ponder the word *freedom*.

What image does freedom convey to you? Total independence to act and think as you please? Being able to be yourself? Living a life of ease?

For some, freedom might mean release from certain confining circumstances such as a difficult job or an impossible home situation. For others, being free means release from a habit such as drug or alcohol abuse. Certain individuals, especially younger people, think freedom means a total lack of restraint, which seems to include a relinquishment of all obligations and ties. To some women, "liberation" has become an almost all-consuming goal in and of itself.

Perhaps former Senator Adlai Stevenson hit on a truth, when he said, "We have confused being free with being free and easy."

A DEFINITION OF FREEDOM

Because the word *freedom* brings to mind something different to each person, it is not that easy to define. Webster defines freedom this way: "The quality of being free, liberation from restraint or from the power of another; independence; release, ease; frankness, outspokenness; and unrestricted use."

Often our personal concept of freedom is not clearly defined in our own minds. In many ways, it is vague and mysterious and even elusive. Ann Bridge, a woman who tried to define the concept back in 1940 said, "Freedom consists of two things: to know each his or her own limitations and to accept them. That is the same thing as to know oneself as one is, without fear or envy or distaste, and to recognize and accept the conditions under which one lives, also without fear or envy or distaste. When you do this, you shall be free." Ann Bridge saw freedom as being able to be yourself. I believe that this is closer to the true meaning than the feminists' definition, which seems to be the total independence to act and think as we please. Some feminists have become disillusioned with the freedom they have won. Even those who have fought the hardest in the battle for women's rights or "freedom" have now begun to ask questions.

Take Betty Friedan, for example. *The Feminine Mystique* was among one of the most influential books of the modern feminist movement and led many women to reevaluate their lives. In 1981 Betty wrote a sequel, *The Second Stage*, in which she appraised the results of the women's movement. Much of what she found was, of course, positive. However, she also discovered some problems. Listening to her own daughter and sons and others of their generation, she sensed something "out of focus," something "going wrong." She said:

> From these daughters, getting older now, working so hard, determined not to be trapped as their mothers were, and expecting so much, taking for granted the opportunities we had to struggle for, I've begun to hear undertones of pain and puzzlement, a queasiness, an uneasiness, almost a bitterness that they hardly dare admit. As if with all those opportunities that we won for them, and envy them, how can they ask out loud certain

> questions, talk about certain other needs they aren't supposed to worry about—those old needs which shaped our lives, and trapped us, and against which we rebelled?[1]

Betty Friedan, along with many others, has noticed a growing discontentment with the feminist movement. Could it be that while seeking and obtaining liberation and opening many formerly closed doors, this movement has failed to take into account other deep fundamental needs that must be met before women can fully participate in the privileges and prosperities of freedom?

Dee Jepsen, former special assistant to the president and herself a mother of six, says in her book, *Women: Beyond Equal Rights*, "The emptiness and bitterness that is so recognizable in some older feminists has been a 'turn-off' for some of the younger women today." She quotes from an interview with several young women in their twenties in *The New York Times Magazine*. These young women acknowledged that they felt uncomfortable with much of feminism, particularly lesbianism, bitterness, and radicalism.

One young woman said, "My abandonment of feminism was a process of observation. Look around and you will see some happy women, and you will see some bitter, bitter women. The unhappy women are all feminists. You will find few happy, enthusiastic, relaxed people who are ardent supporters of feminism. Feminists are really tortured people."[2]

A Frustrated Feminist

I am confused.
I feel used
frustrated,
anxious
bitter too.
Why
do I feel this way
in our day
of liberation?

I am told this
I am told that.

I run here
I run there.
And I hear it said
that it is out there
somewhere. . .
this "being free."

My past haunts.
My present is bare.
My future hopeless,
Oh, the despair
of it all.

The longing
the looking
continues.
I seek love,
fulfillment
and
identity.
I long for
truth,
meaning,
and reality,
but, I experience
weariness,
loneliness,
no hope
no reason to be
and
this is what they call
"Being Free"?

Gigi Graham Tchividjian

Do women today really know what true freedom is? For many years now, women have been seeking and obtaining freedom. However, they continue to be dissatisfied and confused. Why? Some years ago, Anne Morrow Lindbergh offered one explanation in her book *Gift from the Sea*: "Mechanically, woman has gained in the past generation. Certainly in America, our lives are easier, freer, more open to opportunities, thanks—among other things—to the Feminist battles. But, these hard-won prizes are insufficient because we have not yet learned how to use them." She goes on to say that "the feminists did not look far enough ahead. They laid down no rules of conduct. For them it was enough to demand the privileges. And women today are still searching. We are aware of our hunger and needs, but still ignorant of what will satisfy them."[3]

ORIGIN OF FREEDOM

Even Ann Bridge's definition of freedom did not consider the source of freedom. Could it be that we have forgotten that God is the originator and creator of all freedom?

Liberation, in its purest form, was God's original gift and plan for both men and women. He gave us the freedom of enjoyment, the freedom to savor all that He had created. He gave us the freedom of fellowship, freedom to communicate with Almighty God and with each other. And He gave us the freedom of choice, the ultimate freedom. Although freedom was God's original plan, we, through mother Eve, were not respectful of our freedom nor responsible with it. Eve allowed Satan to convince her that she didn't need God (she disobeyed the only limitation set upon her freedom) and she didn't need Adam (as far as we know she did not consult Adam), that she could go it alone. So Eve stepped out of the well-defined guidelines of the framework of freedom and tossed God's beautiful gift into the hands of the enemy. And we have endeavored ever since that day to regain true freedom.

In *Let Me Be a Woman*, Elisabeth Elliot said that "all creatures, with two exceptions that we know of, have willingly taken the places appointed to them. The Bible speaks of angels who rebelled and therefore were cast down out of heaven, and of the fall of man. Adam and Eve were not satisfied with the place assigned them. They refused the single limitation set upon them in the garden and thus brought sin and death into the world. It was in fact, the woman, Eve, who saw the opportunity to be something other than she was meant to be—the Serpent convinced her that she could easily be 'like God.'

"What sort of world might it have been if Eve had refused the Serpent's offer?" Elisabeth Elliot wonders. "What if Eve had said to him instead, 'Let me not be like God. Let me be what I was made to be—*let me be a woman*'?"[4]

Ever since that day, God has been at work to restore that precious gift to us. Since genuine freedom comes from Him, we will not be able to experience it unless He is a part of our lives.

TRUE FREEDOM

Could another explanation of our confusion and unsatisfied needs be that in spite of all the freedom we enjoy, we are still not free of ourselves?

To experience true freedom in all its dignity and beauty, we first must be free from ourselves. This means we must be liberated from our *past* and we must experience freedom in our *present* so that we will be free for our *future*.

Many women cannot experience freedom because of something in their past. For some, it may be a deep dark memory. Perhaps you have such a memory and no one knows about your past experiences, not even your husband or your closest friend. You live in fear that if they found out, they would lose respect for you or even reject you altogether.

For other women, the past holds tragedy. Have you lost a loved one? Have you suffered a debilitating or disfiguring injury, or caused irreparable pain to someone else? Maybe your past has been stormy, and you feel so battered and bruised you no longer have the courage to try again.

You may look back over the years and realize how you have taken the gift of time and wasted it. You know that it is now too late to retrieve this great gift.

So many women are paralyzed in their present because they are chained to something in their past. Only Jesus Christ can open the closets of our past, forgive our sins, and free us from our guilt. One of my favorite hymns says, "All the fitness He requireth, is to feel our need of Him." Once we turn to God and confess our sins, He not only forgives them, but He chooses to forget them. Psalm 103:12 says,

"As far as the east is from the west, so far hath he removed our transgressions from us" (KJV). Corrie ten Boom used to say it this way, "God takes our sins and buries them in the deepest sea. Then he puts up a sign, No Fishing Allowed."

The story is told of a Catholic priest who committed a sin many years ago. Although he had confessed his sin and was sorry for it, he could find no peace and assurance that he had indeed been forgiven.

A little woman living in his parish, who loved the Lord deeply, claimed to actually speak to the Lord in visions. One day, the priest could stand his burden no longer and decided to test this parishioner's claims. He went to her and asked, "You say that you actually speak to the Lord in visions; then would you do something for me? The next time you talk to Him, would you ask Him what sin your priest committed years ago when he was a young man?"

The little woman assured the priest that she would.

A few days later, the priest went to visit her. "Well, did the Lord speak to you in your dreams?" he asked.

"Yes," she replied.

"Did you ask Him what sin it was that I committed?"

"Yes, I did," she answered.

"Well, what did He say?" asked the anxious priest.

"He said, 'I don't remember.'"

Only a sense of total forgiveness can unchain us from our past, and give us true freedom in our present.

Present Freedom

For many women, their present foundation of freedom is unsure. Perhaps they thought that freedom would be found in family reputation or education, or perhaps through personal success or achievement, or even through a husband or social standing.

But in order to really experience freedom in our day-to-day lives we need freedom from feelings of insignificance. Freedom from our many insecurities and longings. Freedom from self-centeredness and discontent, from aimlessness and anxiety and the numerous meaningless activities that fill our days. We need to experience a freedom in our present lives that comes from being controlled by the Holy Spirit and not by our circumstances, our compulsions, or the dictates of our culture.

Our only sure foundation is Christ (see 1 Cor. 3:10–11). Our true fulfillment is found in Him. As Paul tells us in Colossians 2:10, we "are complete in Him" (KJV). We are cemented to Him the moment we yield our heart, mind, and will to Him and allow Him to build our lives as He wishes.

If God has forgiven our past and is in control in our present day-to-day activities and circumstances, then we have nothing to fear in our future. He will be there, too, offering the same grace and strength. I have always loved the little sign above my mother's desk that reads, "Fear not tomorrow, God is already there."

Now that we are free from ourselves, we can take a closer look at liberation.

INTEGRATING FAITH AND FREEDOM

Many Christian women struggle with the idea of liberation. They have been taught that women ought to get married, stay home, and raise children. They are made to believe that anything else is accepting God's second best. So they shy away from anything remotely connected with "feminists" or "liberation." But Donald Cole, in his editorial in *Moody* magazine, reminds us that "many will never marry. Are they to stay home and just go on filling their hope chests? Many will never have children. Are they supposed to stay home and cook and clean all day for one man?" Some do venture forth and struggle with guilt while others choose to stay close to the traditional roles and play the martyr, facing the dungeons of discouragement and defeat and the wild beasts of resentment and bitterness.

Columnist Joan Beck says, "A good feminist is any woman who wants educational and job opportunities equal to those of men." However, many do find it difficult to integrate what they have been taught with the whole concept of the feminist movement. Many think it is impossible to be a feminist and a Christian. They find that much of the feminist movement is not compatible with their Christian beliefs. And they are right. When Helen Reddy sang, "I am woman, I am invincible, I can do anything," one part of us cried out, "She is right, I can do anything." But we were also cautious of such statements, realizing that mother Eve made this same mistake.

However, as Donald Cole points out, many women today who call themselves feminists don't hate men or despise women who stay home to bring up children. They don't advocate contraceptives for teenagers and don't support abortion. If they are feminists, they are good feminists.

We Christian women can approve much that is acclaimed in the women's movement and enjoy many of its privileges which were earned in well-fought battles. What we do find difficult to integrate is the feminist's basic philosophy, which is often a selfish, self-satisfying, self-seeking, humanistic one.

However, in encouraging Christian women to familiarize themselves with the true meaning of liberation and to enjoy to the fullest all the freedom that God offers, we aren't abandoning biblical principles. Instead we are fulfilling them. It would be incongruous to encourage a liberation that would at the same time cause someone to forsake her faith or alter her convictions.

Dr. Clayton Bell, pastor of Highland Park Presbyterian Church in Dallas, says, "Although the modern feminist movement did not originate in the Christian church, the ministry of Jesus Christ's life and teachings and the atmosphere of Christianity have produced an atmosphere in which this movement could grow. If the American woman really wants to be free, she would do well to examine what the Word of God has to say about the nature of freedom."

The Fulfilled Feminist

"Then one day,
I read,
and ye shall know the Truth,
and the Truth
shall make you free. . . .
I am the Way,
the Truth
and the Life.
If the Son

shall set you free
ye shall be
free indeed.

At *last,*
I *am through*
going round and round.
I *was seeking*
now
I *have found.*

I *am free."*

(*adapted from* John 8:32 *and* 36 *and* 14:6)

Gigi Graham Tchividjian

A fulfilled feminist accepts God's will for her life and uses the freedom that He gives her to do her part in executing His plans and purposes. For some that means marriage, home, and children. But many will never marry. Many will never bear children. To want a job or an education or to aspire after the same benefits as men in no way makes a woman a feminist in the negative sense.

Jeremiah reminds us that God knows the plans that He is planning for us, plans of peace, not of evil, to give us a future and a hope (see Jer. 29:11). But all freedom needs a framework.

FRAMEWORK OF FREEDOM

When God gave us the gift of freedom, He placed it within a framework. He also gave us a well-defined guideline for the effective use of this gift.

For example, a fish is free as long as it stays in the water. If it suddenly declares that it wants its freedom to fly in the air like a bird, disaster occurs. A train is free as long as it stays on the track. However, if it demands freedom to take off down a major highway, the result is destruction and devastation. We, too, can only experience true freedom in its fullest if we remain within the framework of freedom. Often this requires accepting responsibility and practicing discipline.

Responsibility

Freedom is not so much a right to be demanded as a privilege to be examined and utilized with purpose. Going hand in hand with true freedom is responsibility.

I have discovered that I am basically lazy. I am not thrilled about responsibility. I have often felt like cartoonist Garry Trudeau, who said, "I've been trying for some time to develop a lifestyle that doesn't require my presence."

Each time I am away from home where I don't have to plan and prepare meals, constantly police and judge kids' arguments, see the mail piled up on my desk, answer telephone calls, or look at the dirty windows, I enjoy myself tremendously. Then I come home and it all hits me at once. The ringing of the alarm clock at 6:30 A.M. quickly reminds me of my many responsibilities. However, if this normal reaction to responsibility continued day after day, it would indicate signs of immaturity. George Bernard Shaw put it so well when he said, "Liberty means responsibility. That is why most men dread it."

Bette Wells, a psychologist friend of mine, says the most frustrating part of counseling is that some people refuse to grow. There is an unhealthy side to most of us that resists health, responsibility, and growth.

True freedom is intertwined with responsibility so as to form a strong unbreakable cord. Author Lillian Smith put it this way in *Killers of the Dream*: "Freedom and responsibility are like Siamese twins, they usually die if they are parted."

Discipline

Does freedom mean the absence of all restrictions? Does it mean doing as we please when we please?

I once purchased a lovely handknit sweater. The instructions for cleaning and caring for it were written on the label. However, I had the freedom to do as I pleased with it. I chose to step out of the framework of the instructions, and I washed the sweater in hot water. It was ruined. For freedom to be enjoyed it must have a framework not only of responsibility but also of discipline.

According to Scott Peck, author of *The Road Less Travelled*, "Self-discipline might be defined as teaching ourselves to do the unnatural." Each morning, when the alarm clock rings, I am amazed at the discipline my husband demonstrates as he pulls himself from the bed and gets ready for another difficult, exhausting day of work. I have seen him exercise this discipline when bone-tired, distressed over family problems, overwhelmed by financial pressures, and even when sick with fever. He does not do it because it comes naturally to his "ease-loving" nature (many a morning he would prefer to stay in bed), but he does it willingly, lovingly because it is his responsibility to provide for his family and care for his patients. Because the Lord is the strength of his life (Ps. 27:1), he has, as Scott Peck says, a "capacity to do the unnatural, to transcend and hence transform his own nature."

Elisabeth Elliot says, "Freedom means discipline. It means doing the thing we were meant for. What is it to which we are called, we women under God? We are called to be women. . . . The woman who defines her liberation as doing what she wants, or not doing what she does not want, is evading responsibility."[5] When God placed a framework around His gift of freedom, it was not for the purpose of *restriction* but for *liberation*.

A Creative Creator

They talk about a woman's sphere
As though it had a limit;
There's not a place in earth or
heaven,
There's not a task to mankind given,
There's not a blessing or a woe,
There's not a whispered yes or no,
There's not a life, or death, or birth,
That has a feather's weight of worth—
Without a woman in it.

Author unknown

God is the creator of all creativity and diversity.

God is not limited by culture or custom or tradition. He is not limited by twentieth-century thinking or teaching. He is not limited by those who would attempt to say that the framework for a woman is narrowly defined. (In fact, I often wonder about those who dogmatically hold to the view that the Bible clearly and specifically teaches a narrow, limited structure for women. Could it be for their own convenience and comfort?) I personally feel that these same teachers and interpreters have a very small and limited view of God. For I find God to be marvelously original and creative. If He has created each and every snowflake to be different, if all of nature bursts with His diversity, why would He limit His ultimate creation to an assembly line prototype?

Each woman is "custom-made." There is no mass production in the creative plan of God. Each woman is an original and her individually made frame will mirror her originality and uniqueness. There are no formulas in God's framework. Principles, yes; guidelines, directions, instructions, yes; but no easy, ready-made formulas because no two blueprints are alike.

God did not create women because of a whim or because He could not think of a better use for His creative energy. He created us for a special plan and purpose, and in the book of Genesis, we are able to glimpse just a little into the eternal mind of Almighty God and begin to discover a small fragment of that plan beginning to unfold. He created women for a special, unique role, in His ultimate purpose—His plan of redemption and salvation. Because, before the foundation of the world, He intended that His only Son would be born of a woman.

God designed a purpose for women from the moment that He saw that "it was not good for man to be alone." How could this be when Adam lived in a perfect environment? He enjoyed the company of Almighty God. They walked and talked together in the cool of the evening, and God gave Adam all of nature, unmarred by sin. No weeds to pull, no ticks or fleas, no grass to mow, no mosquitos to fight; just pure delight and enjoyment.

Yet, God knew that because of the human limitations set upon Adam by space and time, he could not enjoy God in all His fullness and completeness. It was not that God was insufficient for Adam, but it was like the little five-year-old girl who was afraid to be alone and her mother told her, "But, Sarah, God is with you."

"But I want somebody with skin on," replied Sarah.

God said to Adam, "It is not good for you to be alone, so I am going to give you a 'helper' with skin on it."

Some women look at the supportive role as second best, but God created woman to be in partnership with Himself, to fulfill His eternal plan for Adam and all mankind. That is not second best. From the very beginning, woman has been given a place of highest honor in the mind, heart, and eternal scope of God.

If we continue to walk through the history of Scripture, we find a destiny full of diversity and challenge for woman. Sandra Day O'Connor was our first woman Supreme Court judge, but in Scripture we read of Deborah, a judge who ruled Israel and led her nation to victory against Sisera. Dorcas was a philanthropist and Lydia was a benevolent businesswoman who sold purple silk. Women such as the one described in Proverbs 31 were praised as wives, mothers, and administrators. The numerous businesswomen mentioned in Ms. magazine may be new to us, but not to the pages of Scripture.

Esther was a beautiful young Jewish maiden who did much more than just win the heart of the King of Persia because of her outward and inner beauty. She was daring and cunning enough not only to warn her people of their impending persecution but also to expose the wicked Haman. Priscilla and Phoebe were co-workers with the disciples in the early church. Women deacons are not a new concept.

Women also filled more traditional roles, like Mary who accepted God's purpose for her life as the mother of Christ when she was just a teenager. Sarah was the beautiful, submissive wife of a wealthy patriarch. Hannah was a mother who gave her son unselfishly to God's work. Ruth was a wife who devoted herself to her husband and then to his family when she spoke the words, "Wherever you go, I will go. And wherever you lodge, I will lodge. Your people shall be my people." She then spent her life fulfilling those words.

These women fulfilled God's purpose in their lives with creative and courageous acts. They were no different from hundreds of other women who fill the pages of history books and who have dared to accept God's plan for their lives and step out for the good of mankind—women like Joan of Arc, Florence Nightingale, and Harriet Beecher Stowe.

There are many others whose names may not be known to us who also believed they were created for a purpose and used the liberty God gave them to the fullest. Women like Susannah Wesley, mother of nineteen children, among them, John, the founder of the Methodist movement, and Charles, the great hymn writer. English author Isaac Taylor said, "Susannah Wesley was the mother of Methodism in a religious and moral sense; for her courage, her submissiveness to authority, the high tone of her mind, her independence and self control, the warmth of her devotional feelings, and the practical direction she gave."

Susannah gave birth to her nineteen children in nineteen years and was a naturally frail woman. Although she was busy with family cares and trials often overwhelmed her, she set aside two hours a day for private devotion. Mabel Brailsford said about Susannah, "When we ask ourselves how twenty-four hours could hold all normal activities, which she, a frail woman of thirty, was able to crowd into them, the answer may be found in these two hours of daily retirement, when she drew from God, in the quietness of her own room, peace and patience and an indefatigable courage."[6]

Emma Moody, the wife of Dwight L. Moody, the evangelist who founded Moody Bible Institute, is another example of a woman who used her God-given freedom and gifts.

Emma was a beautiful woman with dark hair, queenly and dignified. She was not strong physically and never went to college, but with her keen intellect she received her education from extensive travels, a wide range of reading, and her contact with every conceivable type of human being.

Dwight was her opposite. He was spontaneous, outspoken, and unlimited in energy and good health. But Emma was content to serve her husband as a "balance wheel," a service he often acknowledged. Her influence on her husband was noted by their son Paul, who said, "My father's admiration for her was as boundless as his love for her. Till the day of his death he never ceased to wonder two things—the use God had made of him, and the miracle of having won the love of a woman he considered so completely his superior."[7]

Her husband was heard to say that in thirty-seven years of marriage she was the only one who never tried to hold him back. She made a home for him, shielded him, wrote his letters, handled all of the money, and did all in her power to free him for the work God had called him to do.

Paul paid his mother this tribute: "To you, father owed such an education as no one else could have given him."

A friend, after observing the Moodys on one of their trips to Scotland, wrote, "One day was enough to show what a source of strength and comfort she was to her husband. The more I saw of her, the more convinced I was that a great deal of his usefulness was owing to her, not only in the work she did for him, relieving him of all correspondence, but also from her character, her independence of thought . . . her calmness, meeting so quietly his impulsiveness."[8]

Emma's contributions even extended to the founding of Moody Bible Institute. In the early years of the institute's history, when it was called the Chicago Evangelization Society, Moody became irritated by the continual opposition and bickering of the trustees. He sent a letter of resignation to them, saying that he was "sick and tired" of the controversy and would expend his energies elsewhere.

Emma wrote a nineteen-page letter to the leaders of the society, assuring them that her husband was not opposed to the work of the institute, just frustrated. Then she convinced Moody to telegraph a withdrawal of his resignation. If Emma had not intervened, the misunderstanding could have continued and the entire project failed.

George Sweeting, president of Moody Bible Institute, said about Emma, "Occasionally at Moody Bible Institute we sing James M. Gray's song, 'God bless the school that D. L. Moody founded.' Perhaps we should add another stanza: 'God bless the school that Emma Moody salvaged.' "

Many women have been given a unique task to accomplish and so were imbued with special grace and strength. These particular women are not necessarily models for us to emulate. We are not all called to be an Esther or a Deborah or a Mother Teresa or a Golda Meir. Neither are we all called to be an Emma Moody. But, we *are* all called to "follow Him."

Although some women have had significant roles to play and

others, seemingly small performances, one thing we all have in common is that somehow we all weave together in God's eternal plan. We all have a role, a purpose, and we will all be given the necessary ability and strength to perform it. Not only has God created us for a purpose, but He has also devised the ingredients that have so far ordered the unique circumstances of our individual lives.

BROAD BORDERS

How vast and wonderfully wide is God's framework of freedom, and yet so few really take advantage of all He has lovingly offered us. The writer David understood this when he wrote, "Thou hast set my feet in a large room" (Ps. 18:19); "Thou hast set me at large" (Ps. 4:1); and "He brought me forth into a large place" (Ps. 118:5).

Yes, our borders are broad. They are large and diverse, but they do have a framework and they do have structure.

Yet, with all of the liberty God gives, we are still often found complaining and discontented. Burdened and bored. Are we perhaps too timid to step out? Do we like it safe? Are we afraid of freedom? Afraid of criticism? Are we uncertain of what it means to accept and experience the liberation that God gives us? Or, perhaps we simply don't understand how it all fits together.

How can you discover what God's framework of freedom means for you? Begin by asking yourself a few questions.

First, what blueprint have you been following? Are your values set by the world or are they based on Scripture?

Second, who is building the structure of your life? Are circumstances designing your structure? Are you drifting, not building at all, just hoping that somehow it will all fall together? Are you attempting to build alone, or are you following the Master Builder?

Third, what are your present circumstances? Are you married or single? Do you have children? What are your values? Your goals? What is your financial situation? God is not limited by these things, but He usually works through them.

Remember the bird and the fish. If you are married with several small children, have little education and less money, it might be unrealistic to say God has given you the freedom to be a medical doctor.

Like the fish, if you defy your framework and take flight, disaster will occur.

Although the Scriptures say, "The Lord shall enlarge thy border, as He hath promised" (Deut. 12:20, KJV), God cannot bless you if He has conferred on you one responsibility and you abandon it for another. Although you may have the freedom, it is not within the boundaries of your particular framework.

The Scriptures teach that there are boundary stones we are not to remove. Proverbs 22:28 calls these the "ancient landmarks." I feel that for a married woman these refer to the ancient and holy boundaries of marriage and family. Remember Eve, who claimed independence and freedom and threw her precious gift of free choice into the arms of the enemy. He is always there waiting for another chance.

A married woman's boundaries are more or less fixed. But we should not resent or resist this since boundary stones in Israel's days were not for confinement but for protection. A married woman cannot reach out beyond or go around or under or over her husband and family and expect God's protection. She must exercise her freedom within her God-given roles.

We should be careful and attentive to danger signals. Too much independence for a married woman can be hazardous. All too often, women lose what they hold most dear chasing a rainbow called "freedom." Elisabeth Elliot once again exhorts us to remember that "God has set no traps for us. Quite the contrary. He has summoned us to the only true and full freedom." With the liberating freedom God offers us, we are free to be all that He wants us to be.

Accept God's gift; be liberated. It is not only liberating but exhilarating to experience the kind of freedom only God can give. You may encounter a failure or two, but failure is another form of learning. You may not attain all your goals but you will achieve much more than you ever dreamed possible. And as you allow Him to lead you into His freedom, you will accomplish all He intended for you to accomplish toward His purpose and plan for your life.

As you continue to explore all that God has for Christian women in a changing world, liberate your mind but dedicate your heart, all to the glory of God and His kingdom.

3 A *Gift for* Me?

I love surprises. Just the little phrase "I have a surprise for you" sends excitement through me. Stephan knows this and occasionally leaves a sweet-smelling soap or small bottle of perfume on my pillow. Every now and then I even discover a lovely store-wrapped package.

But sometimes Stephan says, "Gigi, I have a surprise for you."

My excitement and anticipation builds throughout the day and I keep asking, "When will I get my surprise?"

"Later," he replies with a twinkle.

I wait all day, and just as we fall into bed, I ask again, "When will I get my surprise?"

His twinkle brightens and I become a bit suspicious, knowing he can be a tease.

"The surprise," he announces, "is that there is no surprise." Then he laughs and gives me a big hug.

When my sisters and brothers and I were small, we each received a stocking on Christmas morning, filled with goodies. Practical items such as toothpaste, combs, and shampoo were interspersed with candies, gum, and fruit. But, way down in the bottom, tucked up in the toe of the stocking, "Santa" always hid something small but special. A surprise. How I enjoyed the anticipation as I neared the toe. Sometimes I found a small piece of jewelry, other times a bottle of real perfume or a special "keepsake," a sentimental memento from my mother. As much as I appreciated the gift, the anticipation was always the most fun.

We all grew up, and now when all of us children and all seventeen grandchildren gather for Christmas, Santa can find himself faced with an overwhelming task. So it was decided one year that only the grandchildren would receive stockings. My loud cry of dissent could be heard far into the valley below as I firmly refused to give up my stocking.

"I choose to remain a child," I stubbornly announced.

The next morning my stocking hung by the fireplace bulging as usual with a note attached, "To Gigi from a reluctant Santa." (I still get my stocking and enjoy it just as much as I ever did.)

AWARENESS OF GIFTS

You can tell by this story that as a child I looked forward to the holidays, birthdays, and special occasions that prompted surprises and gifts. Then as I grew older and matured into adulthood, I also discovered the joy of giving to and surprising others, but I still gave very little thought to the gifts and surprises that God held in store for me.

Oh, I was made aware very early in my life of God's unique gift of salvation through His Son Jesus Christ, and I accepted this gift at the tender age of four. I had also been taught to be grateful for His bountiful gifts of food, clothing, home, family, and freedom. But it was much later as an adult that I began to discover other gifts God had planned for me. They were joyous surprises.

ACKNOWLEDGMENT OF YOUR GIFTS

"She is so gifted" we often say after we hear an articulate speaker or listen to someone whose clear voice knows no limits. We are also awed by someone's organizational skills or an engineer's technical knowledge. I often marvel as I read the works of other writers and realize how gifted they are in choosing and putting together words in a way that is not only meaningful but beautiful.

The Scriptures teach us that we are all gifted. We are all given spiritual gifts by our heavenly Father to be used for His glory and for the building up of one another (see Eph. 4:12; 1 Pet. 4:10–11). However, some gifts are just more recognizable than others.

Not long ago, Stephan and I were driving along a freeway near Los

Angeles with a couple of our close friends. Suddenly, we passed one of those large green street signs and it brought back vivid, evidently pleasant memories to Stephan's mind.

"I remember as a teenager, driving along this same stretch of highway at high speed in my little white sports car, with the back seat ladened with gifts for my girlfriend who lived not far from here," Stephan told us.

"You never rush home now with the back seat of your car filled with gifts for me," I teased.

"He can't," my friend interjected. "The back seat is already filled with seven bouncing, noisy gifts of various sizes."

Not all gifts are as visible or as obvious as Stephan's and my seven children. And remember, no gift, however highly acclaimed it may be, has a greater degree of importance than any other gift in God's eyes. The one who speaks eloquently is no more important or gifted than the one who serves quietly behind the scenes. (I do believe however, that those who possess the more visible gifts need to be aware of their responsibility—"from whom much is given, much shall be required." (See Luke 12:48.) Many of us think we are not gifted because we use the words *gift* and *talent* interchangeably.

TALENTS

A talent is a natural ability that is usually bestowed on someone at birth. Often it has a special creative capacity, like a literary talent, or an artistic ability to sing or paint, or an exceptional intellectual genius. Those who are blessed with natural talent seem to exercise their particular gifts so easily and naturally.

My friend Michelle sings beautifully, plays the piano almost flawlessly (even without the music), and also draws and paints so well, with seemingly little effort, that her murals decorate the offices of physicians and her drawings enhance the pages of children's books. (Even her doodles would make most art students envious.) Still, she works part-time, cares for her family, and always looks lovely.

Michelle has developed her natural talents and uses them not only to make a living but also for the service and glory of God. She may play the piano for a wedding or bar mitzvah on Saturday, but she is just as ready to play for Bible study on Thursday. She may contract for a large mural or book layout on Monday but be just as ready to illustrate a church program that same week.

Many are blessed with natural abilities and talents. Although all of these might not be mentioned specifically in Scripture, talents and gifts go hand in hand. If God has blessed you with a particular talent, then the same principles would apply to you that apply to spiritual gifts.

As children of God, we recognize that our talents are gifts from Him and so we stand ready and willing to give them back to Him in service. After all, we know the lasting results will be the manifestation of God's power and grace, not our own abilities.

What Are Gifts?

Of course, next to Michelle, I feel very ungifted. I have to work and work hard at each thing I do. Nothing comes easily for me. As far as I know, I have no natural talents, but I am slowly discovering my gifts.

The Bible lists many of the spiritual gifts, such as wisdom, discernment, faith, speaking in tongues, healing, teaching, evangelism, the gift of "helping," of administration, and others (see 1 Cor. 12,13,14; Rom. 12:6–8; Eph. 4:11–12; 1 Pet. 4:10–11). But most scholars today don't feel these lists are complete—for example, music is not mentioned—rather, they offer a sampling of gifts. Another thought would be to assume that these are categories of gifts and that under each would be variations of the gift. For example, the gift of helping might cover a multitude of services, or the gift of encouragement might mean different things to different people. And there are many ways to exercise the gift of teaching and evangelism such as from a public platform or in a home Bible study or with your own child at bedtime.

As you can quickly see, there is almost no limit to the types of gifts God has available for us. There is something suited for everyone. We are each unique, and so is the gift or gifts that God gives to us.

How Do We Receive Our Gifts?

The Scriptures teach that at the moment of salvation, when we become a member of the body of Christ, which is the church, each of us is given a gift or gifts. (See 1 Cor. 12.) These gifts are uniquely suited for us and for our particular situation and task. However, if you don't think you have been given a gift, then the Scripture says you are simply to ask.

During the Spanish War the late President Roosevelt, then a colonel, commanded a regiment of men in Cuba. He was quite fond of his men and became very concerned when several of them fell sick. Hearing that Miss Clara Barton, a woman who devoted herself to nursing wounded soldiers, had received a supply of delicacies for those in her care, he requested that she sell a portion of them for his men. His request was refused. Colonel Roosevelt was very upset. He cared for his men and had offered to pay for the supplies out of his own pocket.

"How can I get these things?" he asked. "I must have proper food for my men."

"Just ask for them, Colonel," Miss Barton replied.

"Oh," said Roosevelt, his face breaking into a smile, "that's the way, is it? Then, I do ask for them."

He got them at once.

We are often like Colonel Roosevelt. We simply forget to ask. James reminds us that we have not because we ask not (James 4:2), and Matthew says the same thing in a positive way: "Ask, and it shall be given you; seek, and ye shall find; knock, and it shall be opened" (Matt. 7:7, KJV). We receive our gifts simply by asking God in faith to give us the gift of His choice.

Once you have asked God for your gifts you are responsible to develop and use them at the appropriate time and in the proper place to maximize their usefulness and effectiveness. Many have a problem, however, of identifying their gifts and so do not know how to cultivate them. We once had a Bible study about the subject of gifts. The biggest problem among those attending the study seemed to be that of trying to identify their particular gifts. First we must identify our gifts before we can begin to cultivate them.

HOW DO WE IDENTIFY AND CULTIVATE OUR GIFTS?

We must first *be* before we can *do*. So, I would like to suggest six "B's" to help you identify and then cultivate your gifts.

Be in Fellowship and Prayer

Only through a consistent and constant walk with the Lord can we discover the gifts He has for us. For example, the more intimate my relationship with my husband, the more I discover what makes him happy, what his needs are, how I can help satisfy them, and how I can help him accomplish his goals. I learn how my particular personality and temperament can be of use to and complement my husband. So it is with the Lord. In intimate fellowship with Him, we begin to discover where we can be of service to Him and how our individual character and circumstances can help Him accomplish His will on earth.

Someone once said, "God's will is the next need I am aware of that I can help satisfy." As we fulfill the needs of those around us we begin to discover our gifts.

A friend of mine with only one grown child had a burden for the children of her neighborhood. She and her husband began a Good News backyard Bible club. They went from door to door inviting the neighborhood kids to their home on Thursday afternoons for Bible stories and cookies. Now they have as many as forty neighborhood children coming on Thursday and they take carloads to Sunday school and church on Sunday. Through this project they discovered not only a gift for teaching children but also gifts in evangelism and family counseling.

Beware of anything in your life keeping you from fellowship with God, maybe an unconfessed sin or simply a busy lifestyle. If something is hindering your relationship, then you must confess it in order to restore that intimate fellowship (Ps. 66:18).

Be Available and Willing

I once saw a book entitled *Beyond This, God Can Not Go*. Of course, I was curious to learn what "this" was and soon discovered it was our availability. God chooses not to go beyond our availability. His gifts are freely offered. He won't force a gift upon us. But we must be open to receive His gifts and then also be available to use them. For instance, if my friends had not been available and willing to give of their time and energy to a neighborhood Bible study, they might never have discovered their gifts of teaching, evangelizing, and counseling.

When I first married and moved to Lausanne, Switzerland, where French was the language spoken, I was too afraid of failure and ridicule to try the few words I knew. Consequently, my French did not improve. However, a couple of years later, we moved to Jerusalem, Israel, where, because of the heavy population of North African Jews, French was spoken as well as Hebrew. Since I spoke no Hebrew, I decided that if I was going to be understood at all in the supermarket, I would have to try my limited French. I did, and through trying, failing, and trying again, I learned French.

A good way to discover your gifts is to be willing to try. Although success is not always synonymous with a gift, it can serve as an indication. You might try to teach a Sunday school class; if you succeed, you just might have discovered a gift. However, if you do not succeed but still have the burden you believe God gave you, try again. *Failure isn't final*. You can fail successfully as I did with French.

Step out in faith and give it a try.

Be Realistic

We all know of people who jump to volunteer for things for which they are unprepared and unskilled; for example, the man who offers to sing a solo and can't carry a tune, or the woman who interviews for a secretarial position but can't type. A friend of mine was having difficulty planning her wedding because her future mother-in-law who possessed only a moderate talent insisted on playing the organ for the ceremony. (I don't know what happened, but they are happily married.)

It is just as important to know what your gifts are *not* as to know what they are. The Scriptures tell us not to think too highly of ourselves (1 Cor. 12:12). In other words, be realistic. At the same time, we must avoid the danger of false humility. Some people are fully capable yet they respond, "Oh no, not me, I just couldn't." This is true of another friend who plays the piano but refuses to do so in front of others even for a small home Bible study. Her false humility keeps her from having a ministry and being a blessing to others.

Amy Carmichael puts it this way: "If I cannot in honest happiness take the second place (or the twentieth); if I cannot take the first without making a fuss about my unworthiness, then I know nothing of Calvary love."[1]

God doesn't allow for either inferiority or superiority complexes. Sometimes it is hard to be objective. I have found that good friends can help you discover your gifts. Friends can also challenge and caution you to make the most effective use of your gift. This was the experience of our Bible study. We helped one another discover his or her gifts and then encouraged each other to use them.

Be Active

It's always easier to steer a moving vehicle. My sister Anne lives in Raleigh, North Carolina. A few years ago, she felt terribly burdened for the spiritual life of her city. The more she prayed about it, the more God laid it on her heart that she was to do something about it. So, although she had never done it before and was scared to death, she went to California and was trained as a Bible teacher at Bible Study Fellowship. She returned to her city and began to organize a Bible study for women. She spent hours in preparation and was so nervous about standing up in front of a group of women and teaching that she developed stomach problems and would actually throw up before she went out to speak. But in fellowship with God, He had laid this burden on her heart, so she was persistent and obedient and discovered gifts she had never dreamed she had. Today she is a gifted, accomplished, effectual Bible teacher expounding the Scripture with authority not only in front of women, but also before pastors and Christian leaders from around the world.

Don't just sit with folded hands waiting for the Lord to bestow on you a gift in some spectacular way. Start moving. He will guide and direct and show you your gifts as you move.

Be Aware of Comparison

My friend Jill Briscoe is an excellent Bible teacher and writer, and sometimes it is hard for me not to envy her gifts. I remember once asking her how she put together a certain Bible study she was teaching that was exceptionally good.

"Oh," she replied, "One day as I was reading my Bible, it just fell out at me. That night, I took my Bible and opened it to the same passage of Scripture and read. Nothing fell out to me."

I was troubled by the temptation I have to compare myself to others until one day when I was watching the various birds that visit our bird feeder in the backyard. I noticed that the noisy blue jay did not fall silent when the mockingbird began to sing. He had his own particular gifts and didn't stop to compare his squawks and squeaks to the mockingbird's lovely melody. Nor did the mockingbird compare his rather drab color to the blue jay's brilliance. In fact, the sounds and the colors of the two birds in my backyard were quite beautiful despite the jay's occasional shrill screech.

Keep your eyes off another's gifts.

I usually feel exceedingly inadequate both as a speaker and as a writer, but every now and again, after a successful experience, I say to myself, "Well, I did it."

Suddenly, I realize what I have said and am terribly ashamed knowing full well that it was God's strength that got me through. So I humbly bow my head and thank Him. We need to beware of assuming we are accomplishing anything in our own strength.

Not long ago, I attended a seminar led by a well-known Christian leader. All day, again and again, she spoke of *her* books, *her* seminar, *her* ministry. She pushed the sale of her books so much that I wondered whether or not her "ministry" was a service or a profit-making corporation. I felt sad the entire day.

Remember: *Keep your eyes off the gift and on the Giver*. It is His gift, given by grace, to use as He wills, for His glory.

Be Accountable

Arnold Newman, the master photographer, once said, "If you are given a gift, it is your duty to use it." Once you have discovered a gift, beware of grieving the Lord by neglecting your gift.

Most of us have read Matthew's story of the talents, but we often have to be reminded of its importance. The man in the story entrusted his possessions to three servants. To one he gave five talents; to another, two; and to the third servant, one talent. The servant who received the five talents immediately went and used those talents to gain five more. The one who received two talents doubled his gifts also. But the servant who received only one talent was afraid and hid his talent in the ground.

The master was disappointed and angry with the third servant for hiding his talent, calling him lazy and wicked. He took his talent away from the lazy man and ordered him cast into outer darkness. But the master's response to the servants who increased their talents by using them is one of my favorite passages in Scripture: "Well done, thou good and faithful servant." He said to them, "You were faithful over a few things, I will make you ruler over many things" (Matt. 25:23).

Each of us is responsible for the gifts God gives us.

A WORD TO HUSBANDS

Because I feel it is vitally important that husbands help their wives discover and exercise their gifts, I would like to put in a word to husbands here.

Stuart Briscoe, a well-known minister and author, wrote an article in the February 1983, *Moody Monthly*. He warned that in this male-oriented society men, pastors, husbands, and fathers in particular have a great responsibility to help women pursue their gifts because one day they may stand before the judgment seat of God and be held responsible for the gifts of the women in their lives. They may be asked if they encouraged or buried the gifts of their wives and daughters.

As his personal friend, I know Stuart Briscoe has encouraged the women in his life to discover and use their gifts. Perhaps this was easy for him because his wife, Jill, once said about exploring your gift, "It is not right to use God's time [fellowship time] nor your husband's time, nor your children's time, only your *spare* time." And this is exactly what she did.

Stuart was away much of the time preaching, her children were small, and she wanted to minister to her community. So in the evening when all the housework was done and the children were tucked into bed, she opened her home for a Bible study.

I have another friend who is a gifted speaker, but for many years she has left her family to go off and exercise this gift. Her husband once confided how lonely he is and that her children harbor resentments.

So remember:

> *You may not take the Lord's time,*
> *nor your husband's time,*
> *nor your children's time,*
> *but only*
> *your spare time.*

MISUSING GIFTS

Unfortunately some of us misuse our gifts, either through a bad attitude, the wrong motive, or poor timing. It is possible to misuse a gift.

A *Grumbling Spirit*

Perhaps you have asked the Lord for a gift, and He has given you the gift of administration or "helping." However, each time the phone rings and you are asked to exercise your gift you complain. Paul exhorted us to do all things without murmuring (Phil. 2:14). Grumbling is a misuse of a gift.

I sometimes will accept a speaking engagement. But because of my feelings of inadequacy or because of the added pressure of preparation and travel, I begin to mumble and grumble. "Oh, I wish I had never made this commitment," I complain. This is a misuse of the gifts God has given me.

If God has given me a gift and asked me to use it, then I must do so with joy. The same holds true for caring for my home and family. He has graciously given me the gifts of a husband, seven children, and a comfortable home. If I grumble and complain about caring for them, I am misusing His gifts.

Misdirected Motivation

If we become proud and think we can exercise our gifts in our own strength, we are misusing them. We are also misusing them if we display them for our own glory. God may have given us wonderful talents or special gifts but if we use them for self-fulfillment only or for ego trips, we are dangerously misusing them.

Overenthusiasm. I grew up not far from a certain very conservative Christian university. The students from this particular school had the terrible reputation of approaching people on the street while they were shopping and asking them such questions as "Are you saved?" or "Have you repented?" and making a real nuisance of themselves. Often people in the area were careful to avoid these overzealous students who probably meant well but were insensitive and consequently turned people off to Jesus Christ.

I once attended a Bible study led by a talented and knowledgeable teacher. Each time someone gave the wrong answer he made the student feel very uncomfortable, especially if this person was a woman. Soon people began to complain and even avoid the study. He had a gift, but he was misusing it. He had forgotten Peter's instruction: "If anybody asks why you believe as you do, be ready to tell him, and do it in a gentle and respectful way" (1 Pet. 3:15 TLB).

Often we waste both our time and our talents when we become overzealous, as one woman did not long ago. She believed in witnessing about her faith at every opportunity. So one day as she boarded a plane, she asked the Lord to place someone next to her who needed to hear the gospel.

Soon an elderly woman approached and before she even sat down, the first woman said, "I asked the Lord to place me beside someone who needed to know Him, so I guess that's you."

She began a nonstop approach to witnessing that only ended as the elderly woman got up to deplane. The first woman never did discover that her fellow passenger was also a believer and had prayed the same prayer.

Timing

Sometimes it is inappropriate to exercise a spiritual gift, just as it is sometimes inappropriate to use a material gift. For example, Stephan might give me a lovely evening gown, but I would be misusing this gift to wear it to the grocery store.

Some spiritual gifts, like my evening gown, must be used with much discretion and discernment, especially the "miracle" gifts. I myself believe in the gift of healing. (I have an aunt who was miraculously healed and her story is in Catherine Marshall's, *Beyond Ourselves* (New York: Avon, 1968) on pages 214–217.) But I have also seen this gift misused. I believe it is a gift to be used only as the Lord directs and empowers.

God may have given us public gifts but if He has also given us responsibilities at home, we would be misusing our gifts if we abandoned our responsibilities to exercise them, like my friend who leaves a lonely husband at home. So timing is vital. We tend to want to bear apples in raspberry season, and then we wonder why we are fruitless. God will never ask us to neglect our responsibilities to begin to exercise a gift.

MINISTRIES

In the last few years, because of an overinvolvement in "ministries," women have come dangerously close to neglecting their responsibilities.

Not long ago I came across a catalogue of "Christian" speakers, singers, musicians, and comics who were available for "ministry." Located next to each name was a picture and all the necessary information about addresses and fees. As I glanced through this book, I was amazed to find an abundance of women who have "ministries."

I couldn't find in Scripture that a ministry is a national organization so much as it is a spirit of servanthood, so I decided to look this word up in the dictionary. I found it very interesting that the word *ministry* is just a fancy word for *serve*.

How practical the Bible is! The gift of service is one that is mentioned directly in Scripture as the "gift of helps" (1 Cor. 12:28). Not everyone can hold a roomful—or stadium full—of people spellbound, nor can everyone teach, but everyone can help.

About a year before my father comes to a city for an evangelistic crusade, a small office with a team of dedicated people work for long hard hours. Many of these people work on a voluntary basis, stuffing envelopes, typing, and making phone calls. When the Crusade begins, they don't receive public acknowledgment or praise. Their job is behind the scenes and often monotonous but without them there could be no "Billy Graham Crusade."

I have often heard Daddy remark that because he receives so much acclaim, he might one day have to change places with these dear folks. "I may be on the back row of heaven," he says, "behind all these dear people who have worked so hard and received so little glory down here."

William Barclay said that everyone is given a task. It may be a task that all people will see and that history will remember; it may be a task of which no one will ever hear. But in either case it is a task for God.

Humbler Tasks?

Sometimes a woman's task may be of a humbler, more modest nature. I know women who would strongly object to this statement, but I believe that, as a general rule, our natures and natural gifts tend to be more serving and supporting. I find this very comfortable since a sovereign God created us as "helpers." Our very instincts demand that we give and nourish; we instinctively long to satisfy the needs of those we love. We should be proud of this supporting role. The only thing wrong with it is society's tendency to underestimate its value and importance.

Grover Cleveland once said, "American wives and mothers, . . . have through their nurture of children and their influence over men the destinies of our Nation in their keeping to a greater extent than any other single agency."

I believe that a married woman's ministry is threefold, as I said in my book, *Thank You, Lord, for My Home*.

First, she has a ministry to her husband. My mother often says, "It is our job to make our husbands happy and God's job to make them good." When a wife sees her job as a partnership with God, as He created it in Genesis, she is responsible to be the support and encouragement her husband needs and to love and accept him as he is—not as she would like him to be.

Unfortunately, too many wives expect too much from their husbands. Remember the circles of our relationships? The first circle is the relationship between you and your heavenly Father. Only the Lord can fulfill you as a person—your husband can't.

A friend of mine who is a beautiful blond married a man whom all her friends described as a Greek god. When they returned from their honeymoon, her friends asked her, "How was it, Charlotte?"

"Well, he's no longer a Greek god," she replied.

Part of our ministry as wives is not to expect too much of our men. Don't expect your husband or anyone else to be to you what only God Himself can be.

Second, she has a ministry to her children and family. Thomas Edison said, "My mother was the making of me." John Quincy Adams said, "All that I am, my mother made me." The formation of character and moral fiber, the molding of a personality, the development of spiritual depth—all the ingredients that make a precious, valuable, productive human being are largely in the hands of a mother. What an awe-inspiring responsibility and a wondrous privilege. Yet we so often fail to realize this until it is too late.

Someone once said, "A child's life is now." Be with your children now. Sit on the floor and eat popcorn with them now. Take a walk and see the world through the eyes of your toddler now. Take the time to teach the little lessons that are so valuable for life now. Encourage your teenager now. Be there, be available.

One day when Stephan-Nelson was eighteen he came home and found me working in the kitchen.

"Mama," he said wistfully, "I wish when we came home you were just sitting."

What an interesting remark, I thought. *He wants to share his day, and he needs my undivided attention even if it's just for a few moments*. I realized husbands must feel the same way. Just "being there" is a ministry.

We cannot underestimate the gift of helps in the home. Watch out for the subtle ways that others try to dissuade you.

At midnight the would-be ascetic announced:
"This is the time to give up my home and seek for God. Ah, who has held me so long in delusion here?"
God whispered, "I," but the ears of the man were stopped.
With a baby asleep at her breast lay his wife, peacefully sleeping on one side of the bed.
The man said, "Who are ye that have fooled me so long?"
The voice said again, "They are God," but he heard it not.
The baby cried out in its dream, nestling close to its mother.
God commanded, "Stop, fool, leave not thy home," but still he heard not.
God sighed and complained, "Why does my servant wander to seek me, forsaking me?"

Tagore

Beware of anything that takes you away from home. Make sure there is no other way and that it is God's way.

I believe that ministering to our families includes ministering to our parents, our in-laws, and other members of our extended families. Although we have to accomplish this with balance and much God-given wisdom, not caring for our family members is a sin. Timothy warned us, "If any one does not provide for his relatives, and especially for his own family, he has disowned the faith and is worse than an unbeliever" (1 Tim. 5:8 RSV). Referring to Matthew 15:4–5, F. B. Meyer said, "Remember that no gift to God's service is acceptable if you neglect the claims of those who are related to you by natural ties."

My husband once had a psychology professor who was of Greek origin. One day, the family doctor took the professor aside and told him he would have to put his elderly widowed mother in a nursing home.

He was horrified and replied, "Doc, you don't know me. Me put my mother in a nursing home? Never! If one little woman could care for five children, don't you think five grown children can care for one little woman?"

I am not against nursing homes. Sometimes circumstances call for such care of our elderly loved ones, but I liked this professor's attitude, and I am sure it also pleased the Father.

Third, she has a ministry to her community. If you wish for a ministry outside your home, just open your door and look left and right.

A card, a homebaked pie, a visit, a telephone call—each is appreciated in a society that is becoming more and more impersonal. Just being a friend to someone can be a ministry. You would be surprised how few people have friends. The other day a friend of mine kept two young children for a neighbor who had to leave town because her sister had been suddenly killed in an accident. This friend and her husband now have the perfect opportunity to witness to this neighbor's husband who is not a believer. One time I picked up the phone and called a friend I thought looked tired the last time I had seen her, just to ask how she was. Later she told me just how much this simple deed had meant to her.

Not long ago, I underwent surgery on my leg. My friend Joy, who is also a nurse, offered to make the hospital arrangements and then personally spoke with the surgeon and even requested a particular anesthesiologist. She then took the day off to accompany me to the hospital and stayed there until Stephan was able to pick me up. Her trouble meant so much to me. Then, her mother who lives in another part of the state, sent me a gift and a note to say she loved me and was praying for my recovery. I felt so warmed, so loved, so cared for.

Single Service

If you are a single woman, you probably have more opportunities for ministering to your community. My friend Carol is single. She is an elementary school teacher during the week and has a Bible study in a detention center for girls on the weekend. She also teaches a group of young girls in her church on Sunday evenings, is available to her friends and family, and keeps a full, busy schedule. But she doesn't miss the many opportunities also available to her for the threefold ministry of a married woman.

Carol does quite a bit of babysitting. She has noticed that when the parents arrive home the mother is eager to hear how the children are, whereas the husband can't thank her enough for taking care of the children so he could spend some time with his wife.

There are hundreds of young mothers who would love to have you offer to care for their children one weekend so they can have much needed time alone with their husbands. In that simple gesture, you can minister to a man (maybe not yours, but hers), children (again not yours), and your community.

I know how much this gift is appreciated since I have received the gift of helps from single women myself. Ever since my third child, Basyle, was small, I have had nine different young single women live in my home and help me with the children.

What a blessing each young woman has been! Each one came to our home with different talents and gifts and the Lord used each one in a different way. One loved the outdoors and was willing to hike and camp with the children. Another was a professional cake baker and gave my daughter Berdjette a love of baking that she retains to this day. Another had the gift of laughter. The worse the kids behaved, the harder she laughed until she often had to leave the room. She may not have been the greatest help with discipline, but she usually broke the tension, kept us all laughing, and helped us put things in perspective. Each young woman had a real influence over my children and will receive due credit one day from our heavenly Father.

However, about eight years ago, I suddenly found myself without any help in a large home with seven children. I tried to do all the work myself and for a while I managed. But, as you know from personal experience, my job was nonstop from morning till night and I soon found myself close to exhaustion.

Each time I prayed about help in the form of another young woman, the Lord told me to call Sarah, the daughter of a physician in Wisconsin, who was about my age, single, and had a good job with the telephone company. We had become acquainted through her family and also through the church we both attended when we lived in Milwaukee, and I could think of no reason why she would want to come and live with us. However, the Lord kept impressing upon me to call Sarah. So one day out of obedience to Him, I did.

"Sarah," I said over the telephone, "this is Gigi Tchividjian in Florida, and the Lord has laid it on my heart to call you and ask you if you would like to come and live with us and be a 'second mother' to the children."

"I'll be there in two weeks," Sarah answered.

That was eight years ago and she is still living with us. Sarah considers it her God-given ministry to help me care for my husband and children and provide me with the "extra" time I need for writing and speaking. Her ministry is the threefold ministry of womanhood. It's not always easy, yet she does it with love and grace. She will never know what an inspiration and example she is to Stephan and me, nor is she aware of the Christlike influence she has over the children or the testimony she is in the community. But she has accepted the gift of helps and uses it for God's glory.

Yes, some of us have humble gifts and tasks, but that does not mean they are any less divine. The Lord Himself chose these tasks while here on earth, and Peter admonished each of us to "use whatever gift he has received to serve others, faithfully administering God's grace in its various forms. If anyone speaks, he should do it as one speaking the very words of God. If anyone serves, he should do it with the strength God provides, so that in all things God may be praised through Jesus Christ. To Him be the glory and the power for ever and ever. Amen" (1 Pet. 4:10–11 NIV).

Whether your gift is mighty or humble, whether you exercise it in the marketplace or at the podium, in the executive suite or in the school room, in the office or at home, your main task or gift or ministry is to be a light in a dark world. The Scriptures teach that we are the "light of the world" and that we are not to hide our light but to place it on a stand where all can see it. F. B. Meyer, the well-loved teacher, said we are to beware of the bushel and let God choose the stand. Don't hide or neglect your gifts. Watch out for bushels that would try to hide them, and let God choose the stand. Let Him choose where and when and how.

"Let your light so shine before men, that they may see your good works and glorify your Father in heaven" (Matt. 5:16).

4 Circles around Circles:

What Do I Do about All These Relationships?

I couldn't sleep. I lay in bed listening to the gentle whirring of the large ceiling fan and watched the full moon's soft shadows dance playfully on the wall. The gentle tropical breeze caused the palmettos to brush against the window, and the quietness of the night amplified the sounds.

Tears filled my eyes and silently slid down my cheeks. I felt ashamed. I had everything to be thankful for—a loving husband sleeping peacefully beside me, seven healthy children, family, friends, a lovely home. Yet I was overwhelmed by the responsibility of relationships.

I thought about each one.

My husband, Stephan, often weighed down by the duty of providing both materially and emotionally for his large family. I thought of how often I forgot to thank him for all he did for us until a moment like that when he was already asleep. I considered how seldom I took the time to voice my appreciation and admiration and how often it must have looked to him that I took him for granted. I thought of his many needs and how I was not really able to meet all of them as I should.

Then I thought of the older children who were in the process of making difficult, life-directing decisions. Stephan-Nelson, our eldest, was seeking God's will for his life, choosing a profession and contemplating marriage. Berdjette, our second child, was also deciding upon a vocation and dealing with options and choices. Basyle, number three, was considering different colleges and experiencing his first romantic heartbreak. Each one needed direction, encouragement, and love.

I thought of the three middle children. Tullian was just turning fourteen and experiencing all the growth of the teenage years including braces, hairstyles, girlfriends, and the tug between responsibilities at home and the natural desire to succumb to the me-generation attitude. Eleven-year-old Aram had his own particular interests and was concerned over his freckles and warts. Although he tended to be quieter than the others, he, too, needed my attention. Jerushah, who at nine was bubbling with life and enthusiasm, kept a social schedule that wore me out. What seemed so small and insignificant to me was terribly important to her, and she had the need to tell me about each day's activities in never-ending detail.

Next, I thought of three-year-old Antony, our youngest, who was growing much too quickly. How I longed to freeze-frame him each week. I felt a strong desire to take more time to be with him, enjoy him, cuddle him before it was too late.

I wanted to be sure that none of these precious human beings was lost in our big family. I wanted each one to be an individual and to know that he or she had a special place in my heart.

My mind turned toward my extended family, my parents, sisters, brothers, nieces, nephews, and in-laws. Each year I made resolutions to write more frequently, call more often, and make more efforts to visit them.

The tears fell faster and I cried out silently, *Lord, I feel so overwhelmed by all these relationships. How can I fulfill my responsibilities to each of them?*

Then I thought of all of my relationships that extended beyond these family ties to our family's many friends. I thought of the couples who were considering divorce and of the friends who were battling cancer. I thought of others who were experiencing the special joys of birth, marriage, or promotion. I longed to share with each one—to sympathize, empathize, or rejoice with them.

Then there was the family on our street who had just moved in—I had not yet welcomed them—and others in our community who had needs, as well as the widows, children, and elderly in our church. Again I cried to the Lord in the words of the poet who said,

Pressed out of measure and pressed to all length;
Pressed so intensely it seems, beyond strength.
Pressure by foes, and pressure from friends.
Pressure on pressure, till life nearly ends.

Lord, I cried, I *feel so inadequate to meet each need.*

The fan continued its gentle drone, and the shadows deepened as the moon rose stealthily in the sky. I heard the faint rolls of a summer night's thunderstorm off in the distance. I could identify so well with the turmoil of that storm.

Exhausted, I drifted off to sleep.

REALITY OF RELATIONSHIPS

There is a scene in the movie *Charade*, where Audrey Hepburn is sitting in the sun on the terrace of a restaurant on the side of a ski slope. She is noticed by handsome Cary Grant. He approaches her table with the intent of making her acquaintance. He makes an attempt to be friendly. She looks up at him with her large black-framed sunglasses, and, as only Audrey Hepburn can, she replies, "Oh, I couldn't possibly make another friend until one of mine dies."

I have so often thought of this and chuckled as I try to cope with all the relationships in my life. My grandmother lived in the same community and had the same friends most of her life, but because we now live in a rapidly changing and transient world we tend to develop multiple, varied, and often complex relationships.

One night around the dinner table, our family decided to count the number of interpersonal relationships there are in our home. Not counting any friends, the extended family, or the dog, we counted more than one hundred interpersonal relationships in our home each day. If we had added one friend who drops by, we would have multiplied this number very quickly.

Even if your family is smaller or you are single, the number of interpersonal relationships you encounter each day might surprise you. No wonder Ralph Waldo Emerson said, "Man is a bundle of relations, a knot of roots." By nine o'clock at night (sometimes by nine o'clock in the morning), I often feel like a knot of roots. I feel twisted and torn, pulled and gnarled, stretched and snagged.

REASONS FOR RELATIONSHIPS

Emerson finished his quote by saying, "A man is a bundle of relations, a knot of roots, *whose flower and fruitage is the world.*"

The world in which we live is made up of the interweaving and intersecting between individuals and groups which we call human relationships. Society exists as a result of these relationships. They provide companionship and communication, and through them we give and receive love and understanding. Through relationships we develop, grow, and learn. And from them we obtain self-esteem, identity, and significance.

Dealing with the reality of these complexities is not new. From the first chapters of Scripture and the first pages of history, we have learned of the relationship between God and man, man and woman, parents and children, brother and brother, family and family, tribe and tribe, nation and nation. Libraries and bookstores are filled with books dealing with the subject of relationships. The social sciences, anthropology, sociology, and psychology, all deal with the various aspects and phases of relationships. In fact, all of Scripture involves relationships, our relationship with God and with our fellow human beings.

As women in a changing world, we need to be prepared to face not only multiple relationships but the varied and changing conditions that exist between ourselves and those around us.

One day Stephan offered some valuable insights into my quest for a semblance of sanity in the network of my relationships. He suggested that I look at the whole subject of relationships as circles within circles.

So, I sat down and drew a circle, a small one at first. Then I drew around that one another circle, and then another, circle after circle, each one becoming a little larger than the previous one, each one representing a different category of relationships. (The figure shows what I came up with.)

Depending on your circumstances your circles may differ from mine or be arranged in a slightly different order, but the principles will remain the same.

The First Circle: the Inner Sanctum

The first circle is that part of us which is eternal, which has a personal relationship with God: our soul or spirit. It is the most intimate of the circles as well as the most important because it is also the reference point for all the other circles. When we become confused or muddled in the other circles, we refer to this small inner one.

I compare this inner circle to the reference point used by the National Ocean Survey, a small federal agency whose business it is to locate the exact position of every point in the United States.

This scientifically recognized point is a small bronze disk in north central Kansas, which marks where the thirty-ninth parallel from the Atlantic to the Pacific crosses the ninety-eighth meridian running from Canada to the Rio Grande. All ocean liners, commercial planes and surveyors in the United States and its environs use this reference point. Even the government can build no dams or even shoot a missile without the agency's using this bronze disk to tell exact locations—to the very inch.

As Christians, our reference point is the small inner circle of our intimate relationship with Almighty God, which is built on the Word of God and nurtured on our knees.

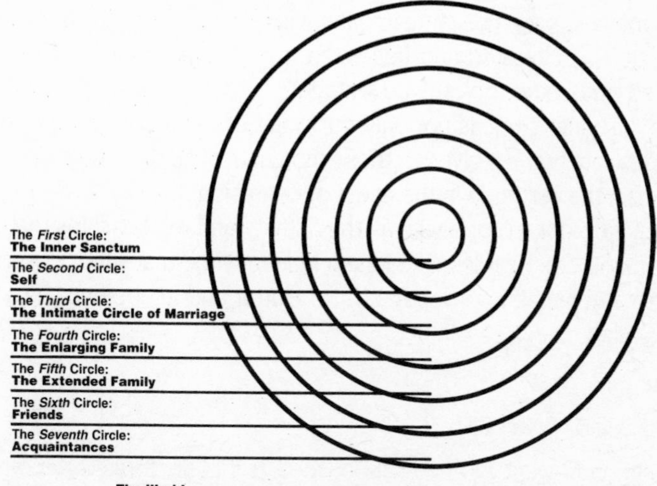

This is the circle we should focus the most attention upon and give the greatest amount of time to. But do we? Instead, this is often our most neglected circle. Often a division exists between this private circle and the others. Because of its personal and intimate nature we tend to think we can camouflage or conceal what really exists in this circle. We are afraid to be vulnerable so we often go for long periods of time pretending that our relationship with God is in order, when in reality it isn't. Often, we are spinning so fast in the other circles that the inner one gets left behind. Our spirit cannot catch up with our compulsive busyness.

"If my private world is in order, it will be because I am convinced that the inner world of the spiritual must govern," Gordon MacDonald said. "If my private world is in order, it will be because I make a *daily* choice to monitor its state of orderliness."[1]

From childhood, I was encouraged to nurture the inner circle. We had family Bible reading and prayer, but I was also taught to have a personal relationship with my heavenly Father. However, over the years I have sometimes neglected the inner circle, either from busyness or because I was "too tired." It wasn't long before my spirit became dry and thirsty and I began to notice a more negative, critical, complaining attitude. Noise, mess, and interruptions became less tolerable and soon I became impatient and frustrated. Because my inner circle was cluttered and neglected, my spiritual resistance was lowered and Satan took full advantage.

This inner circle is not only our point of reference, but it also provides sanctuary. It gives us those moments of calm in the midst of the storm, the certitude in the midst of confusion, that we so desperately seek in order to cope with all the activity and relationships that await us in the other circles. The inner circle must be that which governs all else. Keeping it in order, free from clutter and interference, is a daily exercise.

The Second Circle: Self

Stephan went back to school to earn his doctorate after we had four children. We lived in a small apartment and the only place

Stephan had to study was the dining room table. He would place large earphones over his ears and study with the children running all around him.

One day eight-year-old Stephan-Nelson, seeing his father studying hard for an exam, said, "Dada, you should stop every now and then and rest, or you might get confused."

In this changing world with our fast-paced lifestyles, we, too, tend to get confused. We need to stop every now and then and look inward. Before we rush on, we need to understand who we are and evaluate where we are going.

The saying "Know thyself" is ascribed to many. Philosophers through the ages have wrestled with the problem of "knowing" oneself. We hear references to getting "in touch" with oneself or "finding oneself." We read hundreds of books and spend thousands of dollars trying to understand ourselves better. Although I feel we can get carried away in a sort of morbid introspection and an unhealthy preoccupation with ourselves, we do need a better understanding of ourselves to be more effective in this changing world.

In 1978 we moved to southern Florida. Until then, I had always anticipated and appreciated the different seasons. Each year in North Carolina, Wisconsin, or Switzerland, my spirit had experienced a metamorphosis. With the first cool days of autumn, my thoughts and attention began to turn inward. I thought of sitting curled up beside the fireplace with a good book and a cup of tea. I gleaned magazines and cookbooks for tempting new recipes. I made lists of indoor cleaning projects that had been neglected during the warm, lazy days of summer. As the summer pace slowed and the children returned to school, I discovered more time for myself. I read more. I became more introspective and thoughtful. I began to turn inward and give more attention to circles one and two.

Your time of introspection may not follow seasons as mine did, but I believe we all need to take time to review who we are and where we are going.

One day when my son Tullian, who was quite a little philosopher, was around three, I took him to the grocery store with me. As we walked up and down the aisles choosing the different items on our list, we talked to one another. Suddenly, just for fun, I asked him, "Tullian, what do you know?"

He was quiet for a moment as he considered my question. Then his big green eyes looked up at me from beneath a fringe of blond hair.

"Well," he answered, "I know two things. I know that I am me and you are you."

Who is the "I" that is you?

Many women have an identity problem. Dee Jepsen has observed that much of the disenchantment with the women's movement is that women who were looking for their identities in the wrong place already—their husbands or children—merely shifted the search to their work or careers.

"Looking for our identity as John's wife or Mary's mother will bring disappointment," she wrote, "for John could die tomorrow and Mary could go away to school and make her own life. Then we are left alone without definition. If we seek our identity in our careers, we will find that also will bring disappointment. For one reason or another a career may falter or become hollow and we are again without definition."[2]

Many women go through life looking for identity with a capital "I" and find as actress Jill Clayburgh did that self-centeredness is a dead end. "A woman finds out, as I think so many of us have, that there's finally something beyond this selfhood we've all been urged to achieve," she said. "There's a need to connect, to commit, to have love without rational limits—that all the success and self-sufficiency in the world can't erase."

I am sometimes asked if it was hard to find my own identity when my father is so well known. To be honest, I never thought about it. From earliest childhood, I was taught that my identity was found in my relationship with the Lord Jesus Christ. I was His and He was mine. Any other answer meant that my identity was spelled with a capital "I."

In Scripture we find a paradox. Matthew 10:39 teaches that the more you lose yourself, the more you find yourself. There is such a thing as perfect forgetfulness of self. Psychologist Dr. Larry Crabb says that the greatest block to self-fulfillment is an unhealthy preoccupation with self.

Oswald Chambers, whose devotional book *My Utmost for His Highest* has blessed thousands of Christian lives, said, "Christ-consciousness will take the place of self-consciousness." The more we concentrate on Christ, the more intimate our relationship with Him, and the less we feel the need to "know thyself." Once we know who we are as children of God, our goal is to follow Him and fulfill His desires. We find true fulfillment and identity not in a man or children or a vocation but when we are doing God's will.

The Third Circle: Marriage

Stephan and I had never kissed before we became engaged. (In fact, we had never dated before I said yes to his marriage proposal, a wonderful story for another time.) When he gave me my engagement ring just before Christmas 1962 at the airport in Greenville, South Carolina, I reached up and timidly kissed him on the cheek and said, "Thank you."

He stiffened slightly and said very politely, although a bit formally, "I have decided that we will not kiss until we are married."

I was surprised, to say the least, and quite upset. He would even go so far as to come to breakfast each morning and kiss my little sisters and my mother good morning on both cheeks as the Europeans do, then look at me and say, "Good morning, dear."

I soon sought an opportunity to talk this over with my mother. "How can we build an intimate relationship without some intimacy?" I asked her. "I just can't see going from holding hands right into my wedding night which is just a few short months away."

Mother agreed that intimacy had to grow first and said she would talk to Stephan.

Pascal once said, "The heart has its reasons which reason knows nothing of," and Stephan had his reasons. Now in looking back, I can understand them. Stephan didn't want the physical aspect of our relationship to overshadow its other aspects during our engagement. Being a reasonable man, however, he saw my point and he did give in, and cheerfully I may add.

The relationship within the marriage circle is a unique blending of love, friendship, and sexual intimacy, intended only for the protective arms of the marriage circle. There is no room in this circle for competitiveness or manipulation. Love and loyalty, communication and excitement, fun and tenderness, mutual respect and support—all are part of this beautiful circle.

We have to make a conscious effort to nurture the romance and excitement of the marriage circle. A loving note, a bunch of flowers, a surprise night out, but most of all a lot of appreciation.

A few years ago, we were driving home from visiting my parents in North Carolina. As usual, we got a late start, so we hit Atlanta during rush hour. Traffic was awful and very slow.

Stephan-Nelson, who was eight at the time, was watching the passing cars filled with businessmen hurrying home. After observing hundreds of cars, he said, "All of these men are thinking about their wives."

"How do you know?" I asked.

"Because," he responded, "they all look so stiff."

What a poor commentary on marriage. I was just glad that he noticed it in the passing cars and not in ours.

The marriage circle affects other relationships. And although it is intimate, it is not exclusive. Others, especially the children, should benefit from its warmth and security.

The Fourth Circle: The Enlarging Family

I remember as if it were just yesterday the day I gave birth to my first child, Stephan-Nelson.

I held his tiny, soft, warm form tightly in my arms for fear I would drop him. Ever so carefully I checked his face and hands and feet to make sure his little body was perfect. Then I looked into his deep blue eyes.

He returned my stare, and although I was merely eighteen, I was very aware he was not my possession. God had only loaned this precious individual to Stephan and me, entrusting us to care for him and prepare him for a life of his own. From the first moments of our relationship, I had a very real and deep respect for his individuality and worth as a child of God. However, the responsibility that accompanied that knowledge was awe-inspiring.

In the few minutes it took him to pass through the birth canal the circles of my life took on a drastic change and a cataclysmic shift. I don't care how many parenting classes you take or how many books you read, I don't believe anyone is quite prepared for these changes.

Not long ago, middle-aged friends of ours suddenly discovered they were expecting their first child. Soon after the discovery, a mutual friend said to the expectant father, "Well, I guess you're in for some big changes."

"No," replied the new father, "I don't think so, because we've read several books on the subject."

Of course we "more experienced" parents all had a good laugh.

This fourth circle is a very demanding one: it drains most of our resources, requires large amounts of time, and calls for mental and emotional stability. It exhausts our physical energy, tolerance, and patience. And it requires lots of love and self-sacrifice. Its demands are so great that it is no wonder so many women today are experiencing difficulties trying to balance a career and family.

When the children are young, mothers are forced to concentrate most of their efforts and energies in this circle. We often feel as if we will be confined to this circle forever, and sometimes we feel the walls of this circle are closing in upon us, suffocating us. At these times we must use caution. If we allow ourselves to be pulled in too many directions and stretched too thin the whole structure will suffer.

Our first son was followed by four brothers and two sisters, thus enlarging and expanding our family circle as well as the walls of our home.

Before our last child, Antony, was born, I had a little more time to call my own. The older children were all in school, so I was able to enjoy time with my friends, go away with my husband for weekends, and take more time to write. Then I discovered that I was expecting Antony. (Don't get the wrong idea, he was planned and prayed for.) I tried to keep up my same schedule and pace, but the demands of my family and the pregnancy soon wore me out physically and emotionally. I was forced to pull back within the walls of my family circle. A few people found this difficult to understand and accept. But my closest friends approved and applauded.

We are often under the impression that within the family circle the mother does nothing but give, give, give. While it is true that we are called upon to give of ourselves unselfishly and often sacrificially, it is also true that within these walls we receive more love and acceptance than in the circles beyond. My sister-in-law Jane told me about the time her smallest son came up to her, rubbed her leg, and said in his North Carolina twang, "Mama, you have such paardy legs." It made her day.

In this circle, we receive understanding and forgiveness. Children are great forgivers. After one of the children has had an unjustified tongue-lashing or has caught the brunt of my frustration, I apologize. Their response is usually, "Thats okay, Mama, I understand."

We receive affection. Sarah, my friend and housekeeper of eight years, is unmarried, so has never had a family of her own. She has often remarked, "I might make more money in an office job, have more time off, and a less hectic schedule. But where else would I experience little arms wrapped tightly around my neck, or wet kisses firmly planted on my cheeks, or sticky fingers entwined in mine."

One woman, superintendent of banks for New York state, voiced what thousands discover each year when she said, "My husband and I thought we were happy until the baby came around, and then we found out what *really* makes us happy."

We must regulate the atmosphere in this circle in order to receive its blessings. If we are too busy or overloaded, we will not be in the mood for receiving. We will see burdens instead of blessings. We will sigh instead of sing. In fact, time will pass quickly and we will look back only to discover too late that not only did we not receive but we lost.

I talked recently with a new mother in her middle thirties who had just adopted her first child. Initially she continued to do all she had been doing before the baby arrived. She kept her same work schedule and her social life. The baby cried a lot and she was becoming frustrated. Suddenly she realized she needed to pull back into her family circle. She did. She relaxed, accepted, enjoyed, and, yes, gave, but she also discovered she was receiving more than she had ever thought possible.

The fourth circle is one that is never-ending. It is like the gentle, ever-widening, ever-expanding circle a stone makes when it falls into a pond—the ripples just continue.

The Fifth Circle: The Extended Family

Although children grow up and leave home, lessening our day-to-day responsibilities, we are never free of them. We are never emotionally severed from them. Their cares will always be our cares; their joys, our joys. We will always weep with them and rejoice with them. And when they fall in love and take on their own family circles, we will add their wives or husbands and their families to our ever-widening circles.

I often heard my parents say as we kids grew up and married one by one that they hadn't lost a child, they'd gained more family. Eighteen grandchildren have been added (so far), who have another set of grandparents and aunts and uncles and cousins. This addition and multiplication process continually enlarges our extended family circle.

In-laws. The family circle often offers complexities and complications, such as the "in-law" problem, which has never been a simple one. And the reason for this is that many components make up the family relationship. Social backgrounds, cultural differences, differing educational levels, individual personalities—a variety of ingredients all try to merge and blend.

A pastor friend from St. Martin once shared that when a couple comes together in their home, each person comes with his or her own package from his or her home. For the marriage to be successful, they must be willing to take those two packages and blend the contents into one new unique package patterned after their own flavor.

When I married Stephan I inherited his large Armenian family, his patriarchal father and seven brothers and sisters. At first there was a certain amount of tension. I did not feel welcome, so I did everything I could to achieve acceptance. I adapted to cultural and social differences that were unfamiliar to me. But, bit by bit, things were worked through, and a genuine, mutual love and respect developed.

Also during those early years, Stephan's mother, who was divorced from his father, came to live in our home. Because of her sweet, positive, unassuming attitude, she became my best friend.

Through these years of adjustment, I found that it helps not to expect perfection and to be realistic. There has to be a lot of give and take and compromise. It takes a lot of love and acceptance and respect for the feelings and dignity of others. And developing these qualities takes time and patience.

Always remember that your in-laws are your spouse's parents and your children's grandparents.

Aging parents. Often the circles come "full circle." Just as we were once the most time-consuming and demanding circle in the lives of our parents, they may now require more of our time.

My friend Dorothy's mother became sweetly senile, almost childlike, during her last years, and Dorothy considered it her joy and privilege to care for her. We would often see them sitting side by side in church, her mother resting her head on Dorothy's shoulder like a small child. One day, my friend penned the words of "Full Circle."

Full Circle

We've come full circle, Mother.
I, the parent,
You, the child.
I, the firm authority,
You, obedient, mild.

When the questions are repeated
Time after weary time,
May your voice call back the memory
Of how you answered mine.
Of the patient interest taken
In each project soon begun,
Of the lack of condemnation,
When the task was left undone.
Of your cheerful expectation,
Of your tongue with kindness touched,
Of your only fault I know of
That of loving overmuch.

So, may my words be tender.
My touch be very kind.
Because my "child" has shown the way,
The way I, too, must find.

Dorothy Thielman

I am also the eldest in my family so I feel a great responsibility toward my parents. In the past ten years, my mother has suffered several physical setbacks—accidents, surgeries, and illnesses. I am so grateful that my husband and family not only gave me the freedom to help care for her but also encouraged me to do so. We agree with Dorothy that it is not only a responsibility but a privilege to help care for our parents.

Our circles often overlap and we feel we are being pulled from one to another. Our children are still young enough to require much of our attention or our husbands need more support during a difficult time or our teenagers need counseling and we feel torn. We are suffering ourselves because we are unable to spend much time in the intimate circle. And now our parents are growing older and need more of our care and concern.

William James so well described this state in the German word, *zerrissenheit*—"torn-to-pieces-hood." We cannot eliminate this state altogether, but we can try to minimize it. I found it helpful and encouraging just knowing that this is the norm as we approach the middle years. In *Gift from the Sea*, Anne Morrow Lindbergh likens the middle years to an oyster shell, "untidy, spread out in all directions, heavily encrusted with accumulations."[3]

Do all you can to relieve the stress of these years. I have found that it helps to be organized. It is also important to set priorities, to determine the essential and the unimportant. I have discovered that friendships become more meaningful during these years. Where once I went to Mother and Daddy for advice or with a personal problem, I now hesitate, not wanting to lay another burden on their shoulders; so, my friends have become even more precious. And remember that the inner circle of our relationship with God is our sanctuary. Within its walls we find the grace and strength to carry on; because we can not abdicate, we must go forward.

During these years we need to remember Abraham Lincoln's advice: "You cannot please all of the people all of the time, but you can please some of them some of the time." Or as someone once said, "The sure formula for failure is, try to please everybody."

Be content with less than perfection.

The Sixth Circle: The Circle of Friendship

Stephan and I are blessed with many friends as I have already mentioned. We enjoy a variety of people. My maternal grandfather often remarked to us that we had many friends from varied and interesting backgrounds. He was right. We try to "approach each new person we meet in a spirit of adventure," as Eleanor Roosevelt once suggested. We have discovered her advice was good: "You will find yourself endlessly fascinated by new channels of thought, experience, and personality," she said. We appreciate different personalities, different backgrounds, different cultures, and those whose religious convictions may differ from ours. This has provided us with a broad base for establishing new friendships.

Within this circle of friends we can be ourselves. We can remove our masks because we know we will be loved and accepted for ourselves, as we are. As someone so poignantly observed, "Real friends are those who, when you have made a fool of yourself, don't feel that you've done a permanent job." Within this circle, we find mutual give and take, a requirement for true friendship. We share failures as well as successes. It has been said that "it is easy to forgive others their mistakes; it takes more gumption to forgive them for having witnessed your own."

In this circle of true friends, the child in us is freed. There is laughter and play, there is love and understanding, there is dignity and respect. We relax, we are refreshed, and we receive strength. It is hard to match the rewards of genuine friendship.

Joshua Loth Liebman put it so eloquently when he said, "The primary joy of life is acceptance, approval, the sense of companionship of our human comrades. Many men do not understand that the need for fellowship is really as deep as the need for food, and so they go throughout life accepting many substitutes for genuine, warm, simple relatedness."

As Liebman suggested, we need to guard this sixth circle of relationships. I'm not sure I completely agree with Henry James who once observed, "One friend in a lifetime is much; two are many; three hardly possible." But I do believe that deep, lasting friendships are few in number and comprise a small circle.

The Seventh Circle: Acquaintances

We often use the word *friend* when we really mean acquaintances: business associates, neighbors, teammates, school chums, those we greet at church each week or see periodically at social events. Although our circle of friends is small, our circle of acquaintances is quite large. Someone once defined an acquaintance as a person we know well enough to borrow from but not well enough to lend to.

Because this circle is broad and wide and ever-changing, it tends to get out of hand quickly. We must be careful not to allow nodding acquaintances to take up time and attention that should be reserved for other circles.

Stephan and I have found ourselves making this mistake. Once we contracted with a young man to do some work in our yard. During the process, we discovered that he and his wife were Christians. For some reason still unknown to me, we agreed to go to dinner with them. Now, nothing was wrong with this except that we were already overcommitted. We agreed to take an evening we needed for friends and family to go to dinner with a young man with whom we had very little in common.

Driving home that night, Stephan and I agreed we had to use more discretion in the future. We had sacrificed an evening in circle seven with an acquaintance, thus robbing our other circles. We have discovered that we only have so much time and so much of ourselves to spread around, so we must apportion our time carefully to protect ourselves and the other circles.

The sixth circle can be rewarding and enriching, but it can also be overwhelming and draining. And yet it is simple to avoid these frustrations if we set standards for the circle. On the other hand, we need to be careful not to judge people too quickly. Sometimes deep friendships develop from our acquaintances.

I remember one of our closest friends telling me that after having dinner with us the first time, she remarked to her husband, "Well, we can forget the Tchividjians. We have nothing in common with them."

We all laugh about that comment now since over many years we have discovered that our thoughts, likes, and dislikes are like those of Siamese twins, and rarely a week goes by that we don't enjoy each other's company.

So, once again the circles shift.

Shifting circles, circles circling circles, circles within circles, relationships overlapping and intertwining.

PRINCIPLES FOR REGULATING THE CIRCLES

As I looked over my drawn circles, I discovered I have often allowed confusion within these circles. For instance, sometimes I find myself devoting so much time to a friend that I neglect the family circle. I remember one close friend who was going through a difficult time. For days she followed me from room to room talking about her problems until I realized she was robbing the other circles. So I had to take some practical steps to bring the situation under control.

Sometimes I give out so much to the family circle, that the intimate circle of marriage suffers. Often I arrive at the end of the week too tired to be good company for an evening alone with Stephan. Many a night I crawl into bed long after he is asleep because I have been "tidying up" or finishing a project that could have waited till morning.

Protecting the Boundaries between Your Circles

We lose the balance and symmetry of our circles when we allow elements from one circle to crowd another one. I have learned to maintain the balance of the relationships in my life by vigilantly protecting the boundaries of each individual circle, only allowing shifts and crossovers when appropriate.

When Stephan-Nelson was eight I promised to take him to see the movie *Snoopy*. At the last minute something came up and I had to go off with Stephan. So I suggested that my little son go to the movie with a friend of mine. This naturally caused him to be upset and disappointed. However, later when we arrived home, he said to Stephan, "Dada, I realize now that you and Mama sometimes have to be alone. I realized that when I saw you walking away together." Children can be taught to respect their parents' privacy and need to be together.

Sometimes friends, sporting events, or business obligations violate the boundaries of the family circle.

At the time Stephan-Nelson was asked to participate in after school sports, we were living twenty miles from the high school he attended. So being a part of the team would take more time than usual. He thought long and hard and decided against joining the team because it would mean giving up eating dinner with the family. I was pleased when Stephan-Nelson made a difficult decision to preserve his family time.

My husband has also had to say no to some important, often impressive opportunities in order to keep our close family circle intact.

Be Realistic about Your Responsibilities

Sometimes I find myself becoming totally involved in a problem or situation that is not really my concern or responsibility. For example, my son might come home and share a problem with me that concerns the organization for which he works. I will get all into it offering solutions and giving advice until I wear out. Suddenly I realize I am wasting precious energy in a far-off circle that is not within the realm of my responsibilities. My responsibility ended with listening to my son. It was not my job to reorganize his place of employment.

Psychologists tell us that women tend to feel responsible for the happiness of those around them. I know I do. If someone is unhappy or upset in our home, I am sure it is my fault or at least my responsibility and I will turn somersaults trying to rectify the situation. While this is somewhat normal, I have to realize that I must allow those I love to be responsible for themselves in order to grow as individuals. Sometimes for their own good, I have to say, "It's your problem, you work it out."

We cannot shoulder the burdens and responsibilities of all those around us.

Maintain the Symmetry

According to the World Book Dictionary, *symmetry* is "a regular, balanced form around a center." Our circles should be in their order of priority and importance, and we can only maintain their symmetry if we maintain their proper order.

The center circle—that small, intimate circle of our personal relationship with Christ—is the hub of all our relationships. We can only retain symmetry when this center is in order. If all is in order here, "a regular, balanced form" will be the result of the other circles as well.

If we can say with David, "My contentment is . . . in knowing all is well between us," (Ps. 17:15 TLB) then the second circle of self will automatically be in order. We will experience peace, confidence, and significance. Then we will be able to reach out to the circles beyond—our spouse, our children, our extended family, our friends, our community—and love them as we love ourselves, as Christ commanded.

REWARDS OF RELATIONSHIPS

Antoine de Saint-Exupery said, "There is no hope of joy except in human relations." While we know our joy comes from the Lord (see 1 Chron. 16:27; Ps. 4:7), and that in His presence we discover *fullness* of joy (see Ps. 16:11), we might wonder if it was not for this very reason that when God looked at Adam walking in the garden in the cool of the evening, He said, "It is not good that man should be alone."

God's gift of joy—human relationships.

Additional Reading

The Marriage Builder, by Dr. Lawrence Crabb (Grand Rapids: Zondervan, 1982).

Parents' Guide to the Emotional Needs of Children, Dr. David Goodman (New York: Hawthorn Books).

Love Life for Every Married Couple, by Dr. Ed Wheat (Grand Rapids: Zondervan, 1980).

Raising Positive Kids in a Negative World, by Zig Ziglar (Nashville: Oliver-Nelson, 1985).

Any books by James Dobson.

5 Diapers & Dishes or Pinstripes & Pumps?

I chuckle each time a salesperson has to approve my personal check and asks, "Do you work?"

I am tempted to respond, "Of course I work. I have seven children. I fix three meals a day for ten, I wash and clean, and I buy groceries. I am a chauffeur, a cook, a social director, an educator, a laundress, a part-time gardener, a handywoman, and a full-time organizer. I run an errand service, a day-care center, and an emergency medical center. I am a part-time counselor and a full-time mistress."

But that wouldn't answer the salesclerk's question, which is really, "Are you gainfully employed outside the home?"

More than 60 percent of women today are employed outside the home. They play a very active role in our society, and many Christians have had to adjust their thinking about what they consider to be the traditional roles of women, which is usually housewife and mother.

But has being confined to the home always been the traditional female model?

Cultural and Social Evolvement

In the story of Creation, Eve was given the same injunctions Adam was. Eve was also told to "fill the earth," "subdue it," and to have dominion over all the animals (see Gen. 1:28).

During Abraham's time the fabric of society was largely that of an extended family with the woman being wife and mother and organizer of the "tent." This included many responsibilities, and although she was usually behind the scenes, she often wielded great power.

As cultures and societies emerged and evolved, so did the expectations, roles, and functions of women. And in each culture the factors that dictated these roles were usually of a complex nature.

The late Swiss physician and author Paul Tournier pointed out that during the Middle Ages it was quite normal for women to have a very active place in society. A woman could rule politically as did Catherine de Médicis and Eleanor of Aquitaine. Women were also permitted to vote. Legally they could open shops or start businesses without their husbands' consent. The tax records of that day show that women were employed in a number of occupations such as school teachers, doctors, bookbinders, and plasterers. In fact, it was not until the seventeenth century that women were required to take their husbands' names. They had much personal autonomy.[1]

Nothing New

The "working woman" concept is not new as we sometimes think it is. For years, women have worked in the home, in the fields, and in the factories. Before mechanization, women were very much involved in the textile industry. Spinning, weaving, and lace making were all jobs of importance and were done by women.

In the earlier days of our country, pioneer wives worked equally as hard as their husbands. Medical attention was often handled by husband-and-wife teams. Farmers' wives worked in the fields alongside their husbands, as many still do. Most small enterprises and businesses were family-run, the wives having as much to do with their success as the husbands. Families often lived above the shop, and because of the proximity of home and business, both the husband and wife could be involved with and appreciate the work of the other. And most of these early women had large families to care for as well.

Our Natures

Although the roles and functions of women change from generation to generation and from culture to culture, the basic, God-given, feminine nature remains essentially unchanged. Women are by nature more giving, intuitive, and sensitive. By our very makeup we encourage relationships, warmth, and intimacy.

Dee Jepsen said, "We have, as women, been gifted with greater sensitivity than most men. . . . We have compassionate, caring natures. We don't see numbers and statistics. We see the lives behind them. Women bring a quality to life that men cannot duplicate. We have the capacity to love and to communicate love."[2]

At one time, Dee Jepsen's assessment of women would have been highly praised. But as the world progressed technologically, subtle changes began to happen in attitudes toward the role of women. Society no longer placed the same value on sensitivity and compassion, nor the same worth on being relational and personal. Productivity, competence, numbers and statistics all became more important than the lives behind them. As a result, today we are often more defined by the function we perform and by our achievements than we are by our warmth, compassion, and personableness.

What we refer to as "work" usually means employment outside the home, or family circle. And we find a great concern among Christians over the subject of working women. I can understand why when we are faced with the divorce statistics and when we read that the number of "latch-key" children has topped fifteen million; when we read of the horrors taking place in many day-care centers, the epidemic increase in child abuse and child pornography, and the alarming increase of teenage suicides. We can well wonder if a relationship exists between these statistics and the fact that more than half our nation's women are not at home but "at work."

But it's foolish for Christians to fight over this issue. The problem is complex and arguing accomplishes little. I think we need instead to respect each other's point of view and circumstances and the fact that God has given each of us the freedom to make individual choices.

But we also need to encourage one another to seek a biblical understanding of the issue and then prepare our children to face it as they mature.

Is it wrong or unbiblical for women to want to discover their own individual personhood? Is it wrong for us to wish to develop our individual talents and gifts or to seek employment outside the home?

Perhaps some of us hold to views and prejudices that may not necessarily be biblical. Why, for example, do we consider it not only acceptable but spiritual for a woman to work many hours a week outside of her home in church-related activities? What makes volunteer work so acceptable?

Changes and Choices

I come from a very traditional background and upbringing. I cannot even recall one conversation with my parents or grandparents concerning what I would do or be when I grew up. I was taught early to pray for my future husband and it was taken for granted by all concerned that I would one day marry and have a family. In my case this caused no conflict as I was neither academically nor career oriented. In fact, as far back as I can remember, I only wanted to be a wife and mother.

Now, one might wonder if being presented with more options and choices and more opportunities to discover and explore other possibilities would have awakened in me different desires. Perhaps. I don't know. I made my decision early in life. And although it was based on relatively few choices that I was aware of, I still made it and made it freely. I felt it was God's will for my life, and I remain confident to this day that it was. I am grateful that the Lord in His sovereignty placed me where He did at the time He did and gave me the desires of my heart (see Prov. 3:5–6).

But the world has changed much since I was growing up, and now I find myself as a parent trying to help my children discover God's will and plan for their lives. So I have had to take an honest second look at some of the issues they face in order to free myself from any prejudices based solely upon tradition. As I have looked more closely at these issues, I have realized that some changes have made it easier for women to work outside the home.

Women used to have many children and large families to care for; now in the Western world, the average family has two children and that number is decreasing as more and more couples choose childless lifestyles. Modern conveniences have alleviated much of the burden of housework, so women today have more discretionary time.

We middle-aged mothers who had limited choices for our own lives might watch our daughters discuss their options and feel a bit envious. However, I feel sorry for these young girls. Their choices can be overwhelming. When my daughter Berdjette was twenty-one, she was confused by the many opportunities open to her. Should she continue her education? Accept an interesting job offer in our nation's capital? Look into a lucrative position with a company up north? Or pursue personal interests?

With so many alternatives it is almost impossible to make a decision, and it is often much harder to discern God's will. There are, however, a few principles young women, and older women who are tempted to change their lifestyles, should consider before making a decision.

Let's begin by looking at marriage.

REMEMBER THE HIGH CALL OF MARRIAGE

Many young women are disillusioned by marriage. The marriages they have observed both in our materialistic society and in the church are often disappointing. Many have seen their heroes, role models, and mentors fail in marriage and they're disturbed. They know that one out of two marriages ends in divorce, and many have experienced firsthand the devastation divorce causes children.

The statistics are also against the possibility of their having a happy marriage. One young writer, Hilary Cosell, said in her book, *Woman on a Seesaw,* "A woman could end up the dependent drudge for some man who, if statistics can be trusted, would leave her and her kids six, ten, or twenty years after the wedding to struggle along on insufficient alimony and child-support payments."

Many negative forces are working against marriage, but as Christians, we cannot base our decisions nor structure our lives on society, statistics, or fallen saints. Instead we must live by the Scriptures.

Although Scripture does not teach that everyone is to be married, it does stress the importance of marriage and family. Marriage was the first institution ordained and sanctified by God Himself. It was created for our good and His glory. When God created the heavens and the earth, He said, "It is good." When He created the trees and grass, He said, "It is good." When He created the stars and moon, He said, "It is good." When He created the fowl and the fish, He said, "It is good."

And when He created man, He said, "It is *not* good . . . that man should be alone."

So He created a woman and presented her to man, thus ordaining the first marriage. It took a family to make a difference.

Throughout Scripture we find marriage and family very significant. Upon taking a closer look at Scripture, I discovered that it does not teach that a woman may not work outside of her home, but it does make it very clear that a woman's family must come first (see 1 Tim. 5:8,14).

Proverbs tells us that "a wise woman builds her house" (Prov. 14:1). The apostle Paul told Timothy, "I will therefore that the younger [women] marry, bear children, guide the house, give none occasion to the adversary to speak reproachfully" (1 Tim. 5:14 KJV). And he advised the young pastor Titus that the more experienced women were to "teach the young women to be soberminded [temperate, disciplined], to love their husbands, to love their children, to be discreet, chaste, keepers at home, good, obedient to their own husbands, that the Word of God be not blasphemed [discredited]" (Titus 2:4). Marriage was an important part of the lives of these early Christians who were also living in a changing world.

I believe marriage and motherhood was not only God's original plan but is still His perfect plan for the well-being of not only individuals but society in general. And it seems more women agree with this view than we may realize. A poll taken by the Roper Organization in November 1985, reported that nine out of ten women still feel marriage is the preferred lifestyle.

However, many women will never marry or have families, and many of us will be left alone because of divorce or death. We must be prepared to support ourselves. This may sound fatalistic, but it is realistic.

Choice Is Often a Luxury

Some women do not have a choice; they have to work and the reason is simple: survival.

My friend Carol married her sweetheart in Bible school, and together they responded to God's call to the mission field. For several years they were overseas serving the Lord. One day, he suddenly left and moved back to America leaving Carol and their children behind. He adopted the lifestyle of a hippy and made it clear he did not wish to be encumbered by a family. Carol was forced to live with her parents until she finished her education and was able to find employment.

Betty never finished school. She married a man who had a good job and continued to advance until they were quite comfortable financially. After the birth of her third child, her husband left her. During the divorce proceedings, the judge awarded her alimony for three years, time enough, he said, for her to go back to school and learn a trade or profession. Then she was on her own.

Betty's story is repeated thousands of times across the country. Where once a woman could depend on her husband for financial support, or at least on court-awarded alimony and child support, now she must often be prepared to support not only herself but also her children.

One problem the Equal Rights Movement hasn't solved is that of continued wife support. The ABC news special "After the Sexual Revolution," aired July 1986, reported that the single mother and her children are becoming our new poor with 33 percent falling below poverty level. A woman's standard of living drops by 73 percent after a divorce, while a man's standard of living rises by 42 percent. As my mother says, "Woman's liberation has liberated the men from all of *their* responsibilities."

Desertion and divorce are not the only reasons women have to support themselves. Many married women will be widowed before they are fifty-two, the average age of widowhood. Other women may have to help out with family finances because their husbands have been laid off or are sick or their families have incurred some unexpected expenses.

I believe that for you women who are placed in the position of having to support your family by working full-time and must also care for your home and children, God has made available a special measure of grace. You will experience the power sung about in the well-known song by Annie Johnson Flint, "He giveth more grace when the burdens grow greater. / He sendeth more strength when the labors increase."

I encourage young women today to take advantage of the educational and employment opportunities available to them so they will have a way of supporting themselves and their children if necessary. I also encourage these young women, and also middle-aged women returning to work, to choose vocations that are more conducive to combining home and family. Certain occupations allow more flexibility. Some jobs offer hours that are easier to mix with home schedules, and some jobs can even be done from home as well as from an office.

My friend Cathy is a nurse. After the birth of her first child she wanted to stay home yet her income was still needed. She located a job working for a group of attorneys doing research for medical cases. She works from home, sets her own hours, and makes a good salary.

My friend Cindy owns her own decorating business. Although it is a lot of work, she says that being the boss offers her a lot more freedom and that she can always close her store if the family needs her.

Mary C. Crowley, founder and president of Home Interiors and Gifts, Inc., founded her phenomenally successful business on the principle of giving women a way to remain at home and still earn a decent income, and my sister Bunny works from her home as an acquisitions editor for a large publishing house.

Other careers can be put aside during the child-bearing years and picked up again later. Two of my friends who are teachers keep up their certification, just in case they want to go back to work.

IF YOU HAVE A CHOICE

If you are blessed with a choice, you need to ask yourself some questions to determine your reason for wanting to work outside your home.

What Are Your Personal Circumstances?

First consider your family situation and ask this question: Do we have valid financial needs or do we have material wants?

There is a difference. To me, needs are things that keep a family alive—a roof over their heads, food in their stomachs, clothes on their backs. However nice they may be, no one needs an expensive home in the best neighborhood, designer jeans, or T-bone steaks.

Not long ago, I talked to a mother who had recently gone back to work after fifteen years at home. She said to me, "What could I do? The kids wanted music lessons, tennis lessons, Polo shirts, and Reebok shoes." This woman confused her family's needs with their material wants.

In Matthew 6:25 the Lord told us, "Do not worry about your life, what you will eat or what you will drink; nor about your body, what you will put on. Is not life more than food and the body more than clothing?" I believe a child knows whether his mother is working because the family needs her income to put food on the table or because a new color television or a later model car is more important to her than being home when he comes in the door from school.

The same Roper poll taken in 1985 revealed that 51 percent of the women polled said they would choose work over raising a family. Although all of the reasons were not given, the primary one seems to have been money. Unfortunately, sometimes the woman's salary is not even giving the family that much more buying power. Sometimes she goes to work, and she and her husband later realize that her income has put them in a higher tax bracket.

What Are Your Attitudes and Priorities?

Honestly examine your attitudes. Ask yourself who is first in your life. Has the "me first," "looking out for number one" philosophy taken root in your life? Or are you just bored with homemaking? Often unfavorable comparisons between work outside the home and homemaking make the housewife feel like a drudge. For example, I once saw a television documentary called, "Dishes and Diapers or Pinstripes and Pumps?" Put in these terms, any woman in her right mind would choose the latter. This title takes the worst of homemaking and compares it to the best of a profession.

Do we resent the mundaneness and monotony of our days? Perhaps we need to remind ourselves that work outside the home often involves keen competition and long, frustrating hours. We hear a great deal about the number of women succeeding in business. The truth according to the television special "After the Sexual Revolution," is that seven out of ten are doing "woman's work" with poor pay.

Do we want the independence a personal paycheck can offer? A friend recently told me about a member of her family who took a job and soon discovered an independence that led her to leave her husband and family.

The same women polled by the Roper Organization also said that those women who did choose to stay home should receive a weekly salary from their husbands. Perhaps this is because women no longer find significance in serving. Someone once said, "It is through consecration that drudgery is made divine." Christ never asked us to be successes, but He did command us to be servants (see Mark 10:44). Dishes and diapers can also be a sacred service, a form of worship. Have we forgotten that the Lord Jesus said that when we have done these simple, mundane deeds for the least in His kingdom we have also done them for Him? (see Matt. 25:40).

Are You Looking for Significance?

Judith Bardwick, author of a study of the psychology of women, said that some women have a dual concept of self, which helps to explain their motivation for working outside the home. These women define their femininity in terms of marriage and motherhood, she says. On the other hand, their self-perception or self-image requires independent achievement.

Until a few years ago, if a godly Christian woman questioned her personhood and identity, she didn't mention it. If she longed for independent achievement, she might "ponder it in her heart" but she probably would not voice it. To do so would be to invite criticism and even judgment. She might even believe that to think such thoughts was selfish. Yet many women, including Christian women, do long for significance and feel they cannot find it in the home. Many think, as one young woman put it, that women are fooling themselves if they think they can find fulfillment in a home and family. Could it be that our value is measured instead in terms of salary because our present

him why, he responded, "Because I like it when you need me." I remember hearing my father make similar statements to my mother.

If you take a job, will distance develop between you and your husband where once there was warmth and intimacy? Will your husband think you no longer need him? Will you have time to fan the flames of love or will you be too tired? Will the stresses of two careers take its toll?

Can you take on another commitment without neglecting your present ones? Proverbs put it this way, "She considers a new field before she . . . accepts it—expanding prudently [and not courting neglect of her present duties by assuming others]" (Prov. 31:16 Amplified). If you accept this responsibility, will you end up too busy, tired, and burned out? Will this decision cause you to stay on the edge of a scream?

What about Your Job?

Will you be able to place your family first, as the Scriptures teach, despite the pressure to fulfill the expectations of a corporation or the demands of a business? Success demands a full-time commitment. Can you give yourself fully to both?

Remember my friend Cindy who has her own decorating business? She found herself home alone because her two children were in school. So she decided to try part-time decorating. She began by working out of her home but soon expanded to a store of her own as her business grew. Not too long afterward, she expanded again, moved to a more prestigious location, and hired two people to work for her. What had started out as a small, part-time job to occupy her time and use her talents soon became a full-time career.

For a few months all went well. But then the stress, strain, and tension of family and work began to take their toll. Much of the housework fell to the shoulders of her thirteen-year-old daughter as Cindy found herself many a night still doing paperwork at two in the morning.

Her family often needed her when she already had a full day of scheduled appointments. She more than once found herself dragging a sick child to her place of business or cancelling important clients, which caused her to feel guilty so she tried harder to fulfill her family and clients' needs and expectations.

As the pressure built, she found less and less time for herself and for spiritual growth although these needs were even greater now. Fatigue began to mount, there was less time for love and tenderness, friction built, and soon she and her husband began to exchange cross words. One day, Cindy began to develop health problems, and on the way to the doctor she thought to herself, *Who needs this*?

She decided that something would have to go. She looked at her priorities and responsibilities and put her business in proper perspective. She then assumed leadership in a Bible study and changed her lifestyle. She did what Diane Von Furstenberg suggested: "We must create harmony between what we are at work and what we are as women."

I tend to agree with journalist Hilary Cosell, who said, "I am not sure that it is really possible for most of us to fuse all our roles into one smooth, charming, comfortable, and competent whole." Anne Morrow Lindbergh identified this seemingly impossible struggle in her journal that later became *Gift from the Sea*: "The problem of the woman and her 'work' is still so unsolved. It eats at me perpetually. I should like to be a full time Mother and a full time Artist and a full time Wife-companion and also a 'Charming Woman' on the side. And to be aware and record it all. I cannot do it all. Something must go."

An acquaintance of mine who was trying to do all of the above things—full-time mother, wife, teacher, student, writer—was once struck by Mrs. Lindbergh's statement. She soon found herself in the position of having to "let something go"; sadly, it was her husband that went.

Is all this frustration worth the few extra dollars or the temporary "identity" and significance it costs?

What about You?

What about your health and your emotions? Will you suffer "burnout"?

I read about a well-adjusted, happily married clinical psychologist who works a reasonable twenty-five hours a week. But she stays exhausted.

"Nobody ever told me how tired I was going to be," she said in the magazine article. This woman, who had trained at Harvard and Columbia in the field of her choice, said no one, not even her married women teachers, had ever mentioned to her that it was hard to have a family and a career. No one had ever mentioned the conflicts, the stress, the strain, the depression, the constant fatigue.

Women have tried to become "superwomen" and in so doing have developed the tendency to become workaholics. One magazine I saw put it this way, "The busier we are, the better we like it."

But do we? Many women are beginning to realize the high price they have had to pay. It's beginning to catch up with them. Stress among women is at an all-time high. Many health problems, including heart disease, that have previously plagued men are now also affecting women.

Books on "burnout" have become national best-sellers. I even read of a group in California called "Super Woman Anonymous." It has two hundred burned-out women members, women who have tried to do too much and have given up.

Hilary Cosell described a day in the life of one superwoman named Jane, a high-ranking editor for a national magazine. She makes a good salary, is married, has a small son, and lives in New York City.

Jane is up at six every day. After coffee, she showers, dresses, and does her hair and makeup. Then she dresses and feeds her son, Chris. She drops him off at the day-care center by eight and goes to work. Her husband picks Chris up and is responsible for him almost all afternoon and evening. Since her husband's hours are flexible, he also fixes dinner.

Jane spends an average of eleven or twelve hours a day at the office plus commuting time. Usually she is home by nine. Chris is asleep. She eats something, talks with her husband a few minutes, tries to relax, goes to bed by eleven, and starts all over again the next day.

Jane admits that she stays exhausted. She misses her son and tries to be with him on weekends. But she is usually so tired that she needs also to be alone, so she tends to yell at Chris. Then she feels guilty. She feels guilty for rushing him to grow up too quickly, for making him spend ten hours a day since he was one year old away from his parents in a day-care center. Jane would like to have another child, but time is slipping by. She is thirty-six.

"I'm spread so thin right now," Jane admits, "I don't think there's anything left of me to devote to anything else. I'm an overworked, overtired mother, a fair-weather friend, and a part-time wife. Superwoman, huh? Shlepperwoman is more like it."[5]

Jane's experience is not unique. The cries of disillusioned and disappointed women are everywhere. One employed mother wrote *Newsweek* magazine:

> I felt I was inadequate because I had such a difficult time juggling my responsibilities to my full-time job in sales, my nine-month-old daughter, my husband, our home, and myself. After reading your article . . . , I realize that other women are going through the same concerns and that I should not be embarrassed to say, "It's too much." I have decided that although it will mean a big change in lifestyle, I am going to have to find a less demanding job for a while. My children will only be children for a short period, but there will be many years for me to pursue a career.[6]

A pastor's wife in England confided that she suffered terrible depression. When she went to the psychiatrist, he discovered that she was simply suffering from "burnout." Her husband was a busy rector of a large congregation, and she felt all the pressures of being a pastor's wife. She found herself trying to live up to all the expectations of the church members and bent over backwards trying to please everyone. She reached the point that she no longer enjoyed life and found herself in a deep depression.

The doctor told her she had simply allowed her life to become too full, too busy. He told her she would have to begin doing something each day that she enjoyed doing, for the unique reason of pleasure.

A few years ago, I, too, found myself feeling extremely fatigued and ill. I went to the doctor who talked to me about my lifestyle and took all the necessary tests. He then told me to come back in a few days. When I returned for the results, he told me he could find nothing physically wrong with me.

"But," he advised, "I am sure that if you just slowed down and enjoyed life more, you would soon see a difference in the way you feel."

Fatigue is the number one complaint doctors hear from women, and depression is a close second. Many women try to treat their disorders with medication and drugs instead of a change in lifestyle.

Valium is one of the most prescribed drugs today. Medical writer Maggie Scarf described this ad for Valium: "It showed, as most ads do, a forlorn-looking woman. The text explained that she had a master's degree in fine arts but was living a life 'centered around home and children.' The ad suggested that Valium was the ideal treatment for the 'continuous frustration' she felt in not being able to pursue her vocation."[7] No mention was made of the dangers of taking this or any drug.

Count the Cost

It seems the goals of many women today are to prove they can "have it all" and "do it all." My daughter Berdjette has friends whose mothers have taught them that this is true, that they can do anything and have everything and be successful in many different roles simultaneously. They want their daughters to be "successful" women, but all too often they don't consider the price of this "success."

Does a Christian woman who is not obligated financially have the right to place herself under tremendous pressures? Only she can answer this question. The answer will lie in her husband's feelings and attitudes, her personal circumstances and family responsibilities, her level of energy and ability to manage time, her particular gifts and talents, and her own conscience before God.

Paul Tournier put it this way: "For me to try to lay down the law about the personal choices open to women would be quite ridiculous. Above all, it would treat them as not fully responsible, deny their liberty."

I placed this chapter here after "Are You Liberated?" and "A Gift for Me?" because I wanted you to be aware of the freedom and liberty God has entrusted to each of us and of the fact that those who stay at home are blessed with individual gifts and talents as are those who work outside the home. However, to a large extent, we are free to live our lives as we choose. God has given each of us gifts; how we use them is left up to us. But, as in any choice, the Bible tells us to *count the cost*. Luke said, "For which of you, intending to build a tower, does not sit down first and count the cost?" (Luke 14:28).

Edith Schaeffer reminds us, "Any choice involves the use of time in a way that cannot be used over again." She goes on to say that "time cannot be taken to the cleaner and brought back as good as new, to be used in another way. The use of time is a very permanent thing. . . . Time moves from the present tense into the past tense very relentlessly. . . . Childhood cannot be used over again for another set of memories. . . . neither can the teens, nor the twenties, nor thirties."[8]

One night recently, I was enjoying one of south Florida's famous sunsets. As I watched the large orange ball slowly slide behind the horizon of the vast expanse of ocean, I was suddenly made aware again of how quickly life passes. Another day gone, never to be recaptured.

Perhaps you will choose to give up marriage to pursue a career. If you do, that is your freedom but—will you be lonely? Some women who have put their careers first and have left marriage for later are now regretting it.

A trim, polished executive was interviewed on a television special. She was in her midthirties and had developed a profitable business through hard work and long hours. Now she wished she could get married. But with no prospects and with the statistics against her, she didn't hold out much hope.

Suddenly the interviewer asked, "What do you do about loneliness?"

At first she was defensive; then in front of the television cameras, tears filled the beautifully made-up eyes of this seasoned executive. She quietly admitted, "The fear of being alone is so hard. I will somehow manage, but, no, I don't want to be alone."

Will you one day be like my friend who chose a career and now each time she passes a baby, or watches a small child hug its mother, a sense of longing tugs at her very being? A career might seem glamorous for the moment, but will you always feel so? Will you feel different when it is too late?

Count the cost.

Perhaps you will choose to marry, have a family, and pursue a career all at the same time. That may be your freedom, but do you really want someone else to raise your child? Do you want to give up those precious moments when your child first discovers his world? Or the funny remarks of a two year old or the intriguing questions and keen observations of a three year old? It is so true that babies don't keep.

Count the cost.

There are a few exceptional women who possess high energy levels and can effectively and creatively cope with both home and career. I personally am awed by these women and if I am honest, I must admit I am even slightly envious of them. They appear to have it all. But God seems to have given this amazing ability to only a few, and the rest of us should beware of trying to emulate them.

Remember the Seasons

For most of us, timing and circumstances play a very important role in our decision to "work" or not.

There are different seasons in our lives, and many problems arise because we try to bear fruit out of season. What is right and good for us at twenty-five won't necessarily be appropriate at fifty. Many of the desires of our heart may be met if we wait for the right season.

There is a season to bear babies and care for children and tolerate toddlers. There is a season to quit bearing children and finish raising them (my friends wondered how long this season would last for me). During the seasons of bearing and nurturing, time is usually tight and energy evasive. However, eventually there comes a season to give our children wings and suddenly we discover more time to invest in other interests. Possibly this is the time to once again pick up your career or seek part-time employment.

But, before you get too excited, let me caution you: *Don't overdo.*

An older friend decided after her children were grown that she would go to work for her husband, a busy physician. What started out to be a part-time occupation soon developed into a full-time job. About this time, both sets of parents became ill and needed care. She spent every free minute caring for their needs, shopping, doing errands, and cleaning. The pressure built until she suffered a minor physical and emotional breakdown. She quickly changed her lifestyle, relaxed, and began to enjoy life.

Remember Your Mate

Karen Anderson, the mother of quintuplets, remembers the day she sent her five little ones to first grade. For the first time in years, she was alone all day. Her husband took her to play racquetball and then she wrote, "Eric took me out to lunch at a nice restaurant called The Quay that overlooks the Columbia, where we could watch the barges and sailboats go up and down the river. He ordered a bottle of wine. After the waiter poured us each a glass, Eric said, 'I propose a toast: To the return of my old playmate.'"

My friend Peggy, whose two children are away in college, now has more "free" time then ever before in her life. She was approached not long ago and asked to lead a Bible study which meets two days each week. Peggy is qualified, has the time, and was tempted. But her husband's job makes it necessary for him to travel extensively and he had been looking forward to her accompanying him from time to time when the children were gone. So Peggy said no to the group in order to devote more time to her lover. Recently she told me, "We are experiencing a second honeymoon."

Save time to enjoy your husband. You have spent years taking care of the children, now concentrate on your sweetheart.

Save Enough Energy to Enjoy Being a Grandparent

I had the privilege of growing up just across the street from my maternal grandparents. As soon as they finished raising their own children, they turned to my mother and asked her what they could do to help her. Literally every day of my childhood, the old black telephone would ring and they would ask, "What may we do for you today?"

So many grandparents today are so wrapped up in themselves and their interests that they have little time to give to their grandchildren. I personally don't know where I would be today if I had not had the love and devotion of my godly grandparents. Their back door was always open and I could run in any time I wanted, for a hug or to share my day or to get a piece of chocolate fudge. I knew they loved and accepted me just the way I was.

Stephan's and my good friend Fred Smith says, "The best adults grow up close to a loving grandparent." Save time to be a grandmother.

REWARDS OF CAREFUL CHOICES

I often read Proverbs 31 and begin to feel guilty. This woman was gifted, she was industrious, she was virtuous, she was organized. This woman seems to have been the original "superwoman." In fact, she appears to have been the first "bionic" woman.

But then I take a second look. Her accomplishments were achieved over a *lifetime*, not in a week or a month or even a few short years. She was a faithful woman whose careful choices and creative use of God's time and gifts reaped a lifetime of rich rewards.

Proverbs 31 closes with these accolades: "Her children rise up and call her blessed; her husband also, and he praises her: 'Many daughters have done well, but you excel them all.'" What a great reward! But I can think of no greater reward than this—the final words of my Savior: "Well done, thou good and faithful servant."

6 Where Do I Find the Time?

Today is Stephan's and my wedding anniversary. We have been married for more than twenty-three years now, and today, as I do each year, I allow my mind and emotions to wander back to the beautiful afternoon of May 3, 1963.

I was a young, naive, idealistic girl of seventeen, full of energy and enthusiasm, and I was marrying a handsome, not quite so young, dedicated, Christian gentleman in Montreux, Switzerland. It was lovely. People came from all over the world to honor us in the beautiful seventeenth-century Temple de Montreux overlooking Lake Geneva and the snow-covered French Alps beyond.

Yes, the memories are vivid, clear, almost as if it had all happened only yesterday. I remember the slight apprehension I felt as I awoke early that morning. I quietly drank my cup of *cafe au lait*, gazing out of the bedroom window of the lovely Montreux Palace Hotel, which had been my "home" for several weeks. The lake was quiet and peaceful, the mountains solid and reassuring. A few small sailboats were already dotting the horizon and the large white paddle boat was preparing for another day of ferrying people to and from Geneva, Lausanne, and Evian. What would life hold for me? I wondered. I was so young, so innocent, so scared. Would I be up to the challenges that lay ahead? Had I made the right decision? Had I really understood the Lord? I allowed the questions to come at will.

I looked at my watch. Time was passing quickly. I had a hair appointment, so I quickly showered and dressed. Then I heard a faint knock at my door. Daddy walked in and sat down. He gave me some last minute fatherly advice and encouragement, reminding me that we were all of the same conviction, that Stephan was God's choice for me. He hugged me and quietly left. I waited to get my emotions under control before I faced my sisters and maid of honor in the next room.

The hours passed quickly, and soon I found myself walking down the aisle on Daddy's arm.

"Who giveth this woman to this man?" I heard Cliff Barrows ask.

"Her mother and I do," Daddy answered. He bent and gently kissed my cheek and then gave my hand to my new husband, thus beginning my new life.

Now—years later, as I prepare to attend my son Stephan-Nelson's wedding, I continue to allow the memories and the emotions to flow unhindered for a few minutes. Once again, I ask, as I do each year, "Where have all the years gone?"

Time is shrouded in mystery. We do not really understand the concept of time. Even after reading a definition of time in the dictionary, I am not able to fully comprehend its meaning. Yet, we live and function within the framework of measured time.

Even Saint Augustine, who wrote on the subject of time in his *Confessions*, found an actual definition of time elusive. "What then is time?" he asked. "I know what it is if one asks me what time it is, but if I want to explain it to someone who has asked me, I find that I do not know."

The subject of time is difficult and complex, and the subject of how to manage time is also difficult but essential if we wish to live effective and productive lives.

TIME PASSES SO QUICKLY

When Stephan and I first married and moved into a little house near Lausanne, Switzerland, time seemed to pass slowly; the future seemed long and endless.

I remember the excitement I felt when Stephan first drove me to the little home he had rented for us. It was small by American standards. Although it had five rooms, they were tiny and I felt like I was playing house. I arranged and rearranged furniture, planted and tended red geraniums in our little window boxes. I shopped in small grocer shops and went daily to the bakery for our bread. I washed clothes in a miniature portable washer and fixed dinner for two. Caring for my home and husband was all that was expected of me, and when that was done, I didn't feel guilty sitting and reading a book or just relaxing.

Soon the children began to arrive, and consequently my responsibilities increased. But I still had time to listen to the cowbells in the surrounding pastures or watch the snowflakes fall gently outside my window or drink hot chocolate with Stephan beside the open fire after the little ones were tucked in.

Before long more children arrived. Our house got bigger, the window boxes were exchanged for a larger yard, more mouths needed feeding, and more clothes needed washing. Our circumstances changed, and as a result, our pace quickened, too.

Each year school seemed to start earlier. Then Thanksgiving crept up unexpectedly, and Christmas took me by surprise. Valentine's Day, Easter, the children's birthdays (not to mention my own) came and went and came again. Summer vacation again already? Another year passed.

The day our eldest son registered for the draft a slow panic began to move through me and grip my heart. Suddenly I realized that without even taking much notice this little fellow, who used to play in the fields of wildflowers near our home in Switzerland, was now a man.

I am certain we have all experienced special moments when we watch a child running across the grass and are reminded of another small child who only yesterday (or was it really more than thirty years ago?) ran into her father's waiting arms or sat on her mother's lap and listened to "The Tales of Peter Rabbit." Or as we help our daughter get ready for her first real date, we pause a moment and think back to another soft summer's night that was our own first date. If our daughter happens to glance up, she might see a dreamy look cloud our eyes as we remember our own teenage years and say wistfully to ourselves, *Time passes so quickly*.

Is time today passing more swiftly than it did thirty years ago when my grandmother had time not only for her home and family and church but also for friends and for me?

She spent hours reading aloud to her granddaughters, making our favorite fudge or egg custard, and taking us eighty miles to Gatlinburg, Tennessee, to see a big black bear in a cage drink Coca-Cola out of a bottle. She had time to play Rook ("missionary bridge" as she liked to call it) or Scrabble with us or her friends. She loved crossword puzzles and took the time to make doll clothes for the "great grandbaby." She even had time to sit on her front porch and do handwork while she listened to us recount the events of our day. Every year she had time to enjoy the holidays and wrapped her Christmas packages early, taking special care to make each one unique. She accomplished all of her responsibilities and still had time to relax without feeling guilty.

No, time isn't really passing more quickly for me than it did for my grandmother. I simply became conscious one day of the frightening reality that all those future hopes and plans Stephan and I made in that first small home were now the *present*.

I discovered upon some self-examination that I have failed to savor much of what life has to offer. Precious moments are as fleeting as the beauty of a sunset. I am in danger of rushing through life as a tourist, only taking time for the high spots while the small, daily experiences that give life its character and its most delicious and meaningful moments are all but lost in the shuffle. For me, time is indeed passing quickly and I am often involved with triviality while the important things that hold lasting and eternal value are all but consumed.

When Stephan and I were young and living in Europe, our family was small, life was simple, and there was little to distract me from my strong nesting instinct. I enjoyed life's small, mundane responsibilities. I loved caring for the children, fixing their breakfasts, playing games, reading, putting them down for their daily naps, taking walks in the woods. I found pleasure in folding the clothes neatly and smoothly. I derived satisfaction from seeing the little beds tucked tightly and the table set with care and creativity.

But now I found those same responsibilities irksome, bothersome, irritating. Those small duties that once offered pleasure and significance in caring for the simple needs of my family were now chores. I felt the compulsion to find quicker, easier, and more efficient ways of performing them so I could be free for the many other duties life had sent my way.

I often found myself echoing the woman who said, "I used to enjoy my home and family but now I dread their demands on my time." Where once I had treasured the moments when my children ran through the door and when I heard the familiar sound of my husband arriving home, I now found myself so behind in my work and so worn out that I almost resented the fact that they were home so soon needing a part of my already overtaxed day. I longed to cry out with Alphonse de Lamartine,

> O *time, arrest your flight*!
> *And you, propitious hours, arrest your course*!
> *Let us savor the fleeting delights of our most beautiful days*.

But I could not arrest time and neither can you. It is therefore of utmost importance that we accept this fragile gift and improve our use and stewardship of it.

FRAMEWORK OF TIME

The Bibles teaches that for God there is no time as we understand it. God is not limited by time, nor does He function within the framework of time as we know it. For God there was no beginning, and there will be no end. We cannot understand this, but we simply have to accept it by faith.

In Psalm 90, Moses said of God, "Before the mountains were brought forth, or ever thou hadst formed the earth and the world, even from everlasting to everlasting, thou art God. For a thousand years in thy sight are but as yesterday when it is past, and as a watch in the night" (vv. 2–4 KJV).

From the creation account we understand that time is a created form of measuring finite existence given by God so we can function effectively as an integral part of His eternal plan and purpose. As with everything that God made, time is good, and it is to be used for His glory.

When I realized that time was escaping me, I began to take a long hard look at my life and how I function in this framework called time. Once I saw that time was created by God, for my good and for His glory, then I realized that *time was not my enemy but a precious gift*. The problem was not with time, but with me. I saw that the Lord gives us all the same twenty-four-hour day, but He also gives us the freedom to manage those precious hours as we choose.

INDIVIDUAL TIME ALLOTMENT

Not only was time created by God for our use but He has chosen to limit us through time.

Each of us is allotted a specific amount of time on earth. Ecclesiastes says, "There is a time to be born and time to die." There is also "a time for every purpose" and "a time for every work" (Eccles. 3:1–2). God has provided just the right amount of time for each of us to accomplish all that He would have us accomplish. But Scripture also warns us that the time is short (see 1 Cor. 7:29) and that we are to make the most of the time God has given us (see Eph. 5:16). It is a gift that will not always be ours.

So I began to look for guidelines and principles for using time in the most effective way.

LIFETIME

I discovered that there are different types of time. There is, for example, our *lifetime* which is relative and which Scripture warns us is uncertain. From the moment we enter this world, we are given a "lifetime." For some it may be quite lengthy. The other day our paper recounted the story of a man who had lived for one hundred forty years; my grandparents lived to enjoy their great-grandchildren. For others, it may be shorter. My husband's sister, Asterig, died at the age of four; my cousin Sandy was taken suddenly in his last year of college at the age of twenty-one. In both of these cases we had the distinct impression and the scriptural assurance that their lives had not been cut short but had been completed earlier than most.

Within each lifetime we have a past, a present, and a future.

Past Time

Many people get bogged down in the *past*. Some have regrets and experience the torments of guilt. Others wish they could return to the "good old days," whatever this means. Still others are always chasing the rainbow of eternal youth, spending hundreds of dollars trying to recapture the beauty, vim, and vigor of younger days. (I have been known to spend a few dollars here myself.)

In Scripture I found that we are not encouraged to dwell on the past. We are told that we are to learn from the past, then we are to *lay to rest the regrets and trust God for the results.*

We are also told to enjoy and savour our memories but that we are to live in the present for the future (see Isa. 43:18). Paul said, "Forgetting those things which are behind, and reaching forward to those things which are ahead, I *press [on]*" (Phil. 3:13, italics added).

Future Time

Some get all caught up in the *future*. They want to have a sneak preview and will go to any length to get a glimpse. They fail to enjoy or take advantage of the present because they can't wait for the future. They can't wait to get out of school or to get married or to go on vacation.

Some are paralyzed in the present by their fear of the future. So they sit around like Chicken Little waiting for the sky to fall.

Winston Churchill once said, "It is a mistake to look too far ahead. Only one link in the chain of destiny can be handled at a time."

The Bible paints a realistic, balanced, and practical view of the future. We are told to accept the fact that it is uncertain (James 4:13–15). We are told not to worry or fret about it. In the beautiful sixth chapter of Matthew, where we are assured of God's loving care and provision, we are told not to be anxious about tomorrow (Matt. 6:34). We are to prepare for the future, we are to look forward to it, and we are to trust God for it.

We cannot relive or undo our past. We must accept that God in His sovereignty is weaving all of life into a tapestry that will ultimately bring glory to His name. And although the future is planned and provided for by our heavenly Father, it is unknown and uncertain to us. It is then reasonable to conclude that our main emphasis on time management should be on the *present*.

How can we best use the time God has given to us right now without draining vital energy regretting or wishing to relive the past? Without being anxious about or anticipating the future at the expense of the present?

Time was—is past; thou canst not recall it;
Time is—Thou hast; employ the portion small;
Time future—is not and may never be;
Time present is the only time for thee.
Unknown

Present Time

Usually, the main emphasis in my present day-to-day activities is simply survival. But I am not satisfied with just surviving. I don't want the question of time management to be just one more thing on my list of "have to's." (I even wondered if I had the time to think about time management.) But, since simple survival didn't satisfy me and I had trouble fitting "it" all in, I decided to *take* the time to think about it.

PRACTICAL PRINCIPLES

Nietzsche once said, "If you have a Why, you can put up with the Hows." I had a why. I knew that my lifetime's desire and purpose was to glorify God. I wanted not only my life to count for Him, but all the days, hours, and minutes that make up that *lifetime*.

I knew I could best do this if I was faithful with the gift of time. So I began to look into the whole question of how to manage time more effectively. I discovered that once you get the principles straight and begin to put them into practice, you find yourself less and less often like Winnie the Pooh, "wedged in with great tightness."

In the Beginning God

One day I was talking to my friend Sandy Casteel who teaches a seminar on time management.

"Gigi," she said, her eyes bright with enthusiasm, "the whole principle of time management is wrapped up in the first verse of the Bible, 'In the beginning God.'"

So simple, so obvious, yet I had never thought of it before. God first, not only in my life but in my day and in how I manage my time.

Proverbs 10:27 (TLB) says, "Reverence for God adds hours to each day." We all experience days when we feel like the queen in *Alice in Wonderland*. She said, "It takes all the running you can do to stay in place. If you want to get someplace else, you must run twice as fast as that." Usually on such days, I suddenly remember that I have not yet taken time to seek the Lord's direction and ask for His strength and peace. So I take a moment or two to quiet myself before Him. Suddenly the fog of activity seems to lift and I see things more clearly from His perspective. As I allow the unimportant to wait and discard some activities altogether, I discover that I actually have more time.

The story is told of a certain bishop who had a very heavy workload, yet he arose early each morning and spent two hours in prayer before he started his day. He not only got everything done each day, but he did it well.

One day an added responsibility of great importance was laid upon him. He threw himself into the project and accomplished all he had to do without seeming tired or harried and without neglecting his previous duties and responsibilities. His friends watched in amazement and finally asked him how he was able to do it.

His answer was quite simple. "The more I have to do," he said, "the more I pray. I just rise a bit earlier each morning and everything else I must do during the day seems to take care of itself." This bishop followed the principle, "In the beginning God."

Eternity's Perspective

The second principle is to look at time management from the viewpoint of eternity, from God's perspective. Before becoming involved with something, simply ask how urgent and significant it is from the perspective of eternity.

From God's perspective, it might be more important to read to a child than to keep the house so spotless; to seek new ways to meet your husband's needs than to be on that committee; to continue caring for your home and family than to take that job which would provide extra income for a few luxuries. From God's perspective, attitude is often more important than action. It is more important to be kind, loving, and pleasant than to accomplish much or achieve great things.

Sometimes I am asked what is the most important thing I have learned from my daddy. Without hesitation, I say, "Trying to see things from God's perspective, with eternity's values in view." The lyrics of one of his favorite choruses go like this, "With eternity's values in view, Lord, let me do each day's work for Jesus, with eternity's values in view."

Goals

With the "eternity" principle in mind, we need to establish lifetime goals. Having a purpose in life and then setting goals, both long-term and short-term goals, is very important.

Ted Engstrom, who has for many years led "Managing Your Time" seminars, says that, "A purpose is the general aim that you are going toward, whereas a goal is measurable."

Candi is a songwriter, performer, teacher, and disc jockey. In a recent interview she tells how one day two friends challenged her convictions.

"What is the purpose of your life?" they asked.

"To be a great songwriter and singer, and have some positive influence on others," Candi replied.

Her friends answered, "Candi, those are good goals, but what about your *purpose*?"

Candi could not answer.[1]

My purpose in life is to glorify God. I feel I can do this through writing, my general aim. However, to finish this book by September is my long-term goal and to complete this chapter by Friday is my short-term goal. These goals have definite measurable time frames.

Each one of us needs to ask first what our general purpose or aim in life is and then how we can set long- and short-term goals in order to accomplish this purpose. Then we need to take our list of goals and arrange them in order of importance with eternity's values in view.

Priorities

When I wrote about priorities in A *Woman's Quest for Serenity*, I said that the number one enemy of my personal priority list was busyness.

From the response I received to this chapter, I quickly discovered I was not alone. Busyness has become a way of life for most of us and a compulsion for many. It is a continual battle not to become overcommitted. When our days and hours are too full, we lose sight of what is truly important and we soon forget our priorities in the shuffle.

The other day a neighbor sent a message that she had something to show me. Would I come over to her house for a minute? I was working, so I didn't get the message until dinnertime. The next day I awoke feeling under the weather, and I had a secretary coming to do some work. At three o'clock I was leaving to go out of town for two days. As I was driving up the freeway, I suddenly realized I had not gone to my neighbor's house. People come before things, including deadlines on manuscripts. However, I had allowed myself to become so pressed for time that my priorities became confused.

Being too busy fragments our time, our emotions, our relationships, and soon we lose our grip. We must learn to weigh carefully the value of activities we are asked to participate in, so we will not wander too far from our priorities. If we are not careful and attentive, our lives will soon resemble the garden hose with many holes. It sprays a little water in many different directions but loses its main thrust of power and strength.

Charles Spurgeon once said, "Learn to say no. It will do you more good than being able to speak Latin." Today, we may not have a need for Latin, but the point is well taken.

My friend Sandy, who teaches a time-management seminar, teaches the women who attend to say no. She tells them to place their tongues on the roof of their mouths and then say, "NO." Gordon MacDonald once said, "I have learned to say no to some good things in order to be free for the best."

Balance

Someone once asked me what the hardest thing was about living the Christian life. I answered immediately, "Balance." For example, my mother once said that she didn't work well under pressure but that she didn't work at all without it. The solution? Balance.

Scripture teaches that we are to be "workmen that needeth not to be ashamed" (2 Tim. 2:15, KJV) and that we are to "occupy till [He] comes" (Luke 19:13 KJV). So I firmly believe in activity, achievements, and accomplishments. As with so much else in life, the key is balance. We have already discussed the dangers of being too busy. The answer? Balance, which largely depends on your circumstances, your physical strength and abilities, and your mental and emotional stability.

Balance means weighing the pros and cons, it means judging and deciding what, which, where, and when. Balance is learning to make choices and decisions. Most important, balance is bringing harmony and proportion to your life.

Within the Framework

The next principle follows closely on the heels of priorities: remaining within the framework of our God-given circumstances, potential, and possibilities.

I have often fallen into the trap of comparing myself to someone else, even trying at times to emulate them. What was more important was discovering my own potential. What are your personal circumstances? Your likes and dislikes? What gifts do you have? Set your goals within this framework of God-given possibilities.

Kathy was at her wit's end. She worked with young people in a national Christian organization, but she was miserable. She felt inadequate and frustrated. Many well-meaning friends told her she had to have a spiritual problem, so she spent many hours reading her Bible, praying, and searching her heart. Discouraged and desperate, she talked with someone who realized she was trying to function outside the framework of the potential God had given her. Together they discussed her purpose and aim. Then they began to discover what she enjoyed in life. What activities brought her joy and fulfillment? Where did she feel comfortable and productive? Finally they discussed goals and how she could achieve them. Kathy left youth work and went into a completely different field of activity. Soon she was functioning within the framework God had planned and equipped her for. She began to set and to achieve goals and became effective and useful as the burden of not being able to measure up was lifted.

To be truly fulfilled and effective, we must discover the unique potential and possibilities that make up our individual framework and then remain within its limits, keeping in mind that the framework can change or adjust over the years.

Turning Frustration into Fruitfulness

Effective time management is being *realistic about timing.*

When my daughter, Berdjette, was sixteen, she shared with me just how much Ecclesiastes 3:1 meant to her: "To everything there is a season, and a time to every purpose."

"Mother," she said, "I find that this verse of Ecclesiastes has a lot to do with patience. It says there is a time for everything, but often we want it in *our* time and not God's time. For example, I would love to be finished with school and married with a family, but I realize that this is not God's will now. It is His will that I continue with my studies." She went on to tell me that this passage had taught her a lot about God's perfect timing.

Effective time management is *accepting God's timing.*

If it is impossible now to accomplish your long-term goals, don't be discouraged. Relax, enjoy the "now," and "praise and pray and peg away" at the short-term goals.

My little girl used to sing: "It's raining, it's pouring. The old man is snoring and he bumped into the morning." That is just how I feel many mornings. My first goal each day is to get out of bed to the coffee pot. Usually I feel that I have bumped into the morning. After I have done all that is necessary to get my husband off to his office and the children out the door to school, I like to see what has been "planned" for my day.

Remarkable Time. Each month I take the calendar and mark all the events that are "have to's"—any trips, speaking engagements, out-of-town company, school events, chapter deadlines, special days, and social events (making sure all birthdays, anniversaries and special family days are well marked). Then, I take each week and mark down all I need to do that week.

I call this "Re-*markable* Time," a closer look at all the scheduled events of the month plus the weekly and daily activities: grocery shopping, dental appointments, looking for a special dress for my daughter, lunch with someone who needs my advice.

Restful Time. I try to allow at least one day a week for fun. Lunch with a special friend, shopping for me, an afternoon at the beach, or just sitting in the backyard and reading. I call this "restful time."

Realistic Time. I then try to divide my days into morning and afternoon segments. I like to call this "realistic time" because I try to be as realistic about my goals as possible. I might want to clean all the closets in one morning segment, but the chances of really completing the task are slim; if I allow only one morning segment for this, I will soon find myself irritable and totally frustrated. So I try to be realistic, allowing for the inevitable interruptions and sidetracks plus a little time for me to gather my thoughts together before the family arrive hungry for dinner.

Redeeming Time. The Scriptures tell us to *redeem the time* (Eph. 5:16; Col. 4:5). Time is expendable as one unknown author claimed in the following verse:

> *I have just a minute . . . with sixty seconds in it . . . forced upon me . . .*
> *can't refuse it . . . didn't seek it . . . didn't choose it . . . but it's up to*
> *me to use it . . .*
> *I must suffer if I lose it . . . give account if I abuse it.*
> *Just a tiny little minute . . . but Eternity is in it.*

We cannot go back and experience time again, nor can we arrest time, but with some careful attention, we can redeem time.

Waiting in doctors' offices can be irritating and a loss of precious time unless we go with the attitude that there is really nothing we can do about it; so, we should relax and read a magazine that perhaps we might not have time to read at home, or write a letter that is long overdue. I always try to have with me a good book or magazine to read or a notebook to write in wherever I go. Waiting in line at the bank or for the children after school, I often jot down ideas. I call this redeeming time. These very short periods of time can redeem hours during a week.

We cannot live over again moments that are lost or wasted, but if we are mindful and attentive, conscientious and diligent, we can catch ourselves and thus redeem the time so that later we will not look back upon what Shakespeare referred to as "chronicles of wasted time."

Last Christmas I told the children they could make cookies. I left them in the kitchen for a few moments, and when I returned there was flour and sugar everywhere. Two-year-old Antony was standing in a chair covered from head to toe with cookie dough. My first reaction was frustration at the mess I would have to clean up, then I caught myself just in time from making the mistake that playwright Christopher Fry refers to as, "remarkably losing eternity in the passing moment." I decided that making Christmas cookies with my children builds memories and has much more eternal significance than a clean kitchen. So I laughed and joined in the fun, redeeming what could have been an unpleasant memory and a wasted afternoon.

I once read an interview with O. Wayne Rollins, chairman of the board and chief executive officer of Rollins, Inc., in which he told of his grandmother's resourceful ways to redeem time. "We lived on a hill with a spring at the bottom where the road and the barn were," he said. "Any time any of us went down that hill, for any reason, we had to take two empty buckets down the hill with us to the spring. When she heard us coming back later, she'd ask, 'Did you bring the water?' She never had to send anyone to the spring for water."

She also taught him that time is a precious commodity and that since everyone has twenty-four hours in a day, the success of anyone depends upon how well he or she uses those hours.

Getting Organized

Often when I say, "I don't have the time," I really mean that I don't want to make the time. We can always make time for the things we really want to do. Let's face it, some things we just don't want to do.

Making lists, setting goals, planning our days, weeks, and months helps us face reality. When lists are staring us in the face, we know they need to be done. They keep us from procrastinating and help us stay on top.

Procrastination is often the result of being overwhelmed. We just don't know where to start. Organization helps us to get started and to do one thing at a time. Then we tend to stay on top. We're freed from the needless worry over little details that affect our days.

Little Things Count

Years ago my mother-in-law taught me to set the table early for dinner. "It's one less thing to be done at the most hectic time of day," she used to say, and "It encourages those who come in hungry to see a set table." Since I am not a morning person, one of the children's jobs is to set the breakfast table after dinner which is a big help to me in the morning.

Having a large household and a large home, I am forced to be somewhat organized. I can't clean the entire house in one morning (although I must admit I have tried) so I have divided the house into sections. I keep a list of the duties in each section on the back of the china closet, and each day a specific section gets attacked. This way the house gets cleaned at least once a week. I have found that keeping a broom and mop at each end of our one-story home helps save steps and frustration. Having sponges, cleanser, and a dust pan in each bathroom helps to "keep up" with the mess. Also, our laundry room is far from the bedrooms; so, like O. Wayne Rollins, I try to take a load of folded clothes with me each time I know I'll be near the laundry room.

There are innumerable tips for better organizing a household and thereby redeeming time. Discovering those that are best suited for your needs can be a creative opportunity.

Reasonable Time. The Scriptures speak of "reasonable service." This means not overdoing it but *using small portions of time to get large things accomplished* a little bit at a time.

I have a friend who keeps putting off major cleaning projects because she sees them as giants. Many chores and projects *are* giants if attacked all at once, but though it may take a whole day to wash all the windows in my house, it only takes a few minutes to wash the ones in the living room. So while I wait for the cookies to bake or for a friend who is late, I take a cloth and clean a window or two. They may not sparkle all at the same time, but at least they do get washed and I'm not overwhelmed.

My husband often comes home late for dinner. I used to get very irritated until I realized it didn't bring him home any earlier and that instead my being upset often ruined the rest of the evening. I decided to use these moments to relax or watch the evening news or get ahead by bathing the little ones before supper. Dinner might get a bit overcooked, but I'm less tense and the evening is much more pleasant.

The Bible says to let your "sweet reasonableness be known unto all men" (Phil. 4:5). In order to be sweet at home, I must be *reasonable* about the use of time. When I become too disorganized, too busy, or too tired, the mood of the whole family changes. Everyone tends to be more tense, more nervous, more cross. The woman sets the tone since she is the heart of the home. While this may seem unfair, it's reality.

Time Robbers

In their book, *Managing Your Time*, Dr. Ted Engstrom and R. Alec Mackenzie mention these five "time robbers": inefficiency, indecision, a tension environment, overcommunication, and overconcern. I personally fall short in each of these areas. And while they affect us all, I can't help thinking we women are especially susceptible to them. Think about it. Is changing your mind a woman's prerogative or a time robber? Is overcommunication friendliness or just plain talking too much?

Overconcern? My husband, a psychologist, says that it is the women, the mothers, who tend to become overly concerned and worried. I know I do. Whether it is a teenager out until midnight, a sixteen year old driving the family car for the first time, a room that is in disorder, or table manners, I sometimes tend to be overly concerned.

Efficiency is important and organization very helpful but for a busy wife and mother time management often means simply doing the best you can—aiming for efficiency, trying to be organized, and yet remaining flexible and adaptable. Stuart Briscoe said, "Don't be so flexible that you flop, nor so stiff that you snap."

Growing up in a large, busy, often hectic household, I observed how my mother coped with all of us and with Daddy, whose friends used to say teasingly, "He has the cleanest mind around because he changes it so often." Mother was often forced to make last-minute changes and adjustments and to be incredibly adaptable. Her favorite time management slogans were "Play it by ear" and "Hang loose," which caused us to teasingly call her a very "loose woman."

If Plan A fails, just go on to Plan B. Some days in our home, Plans C and D also fail and we end up at McDonalds.

I often encounter women who are "just" housewives and mothers. They tend to suffer from low self-esteem because they are not "successful" or "high achievers." If you got out of bed this morning, fixed breakfast for your family, then packed the lunches, got your husband off to work, ushered the children out the door in time for school, making sure their teeth were brushed and their hair combed; if you then got dressed, cleaned the kitchen, straightened the rooms, and did the laundry; if you grocery shopped, ran errands, returned home to clean the house and put the wash in the dryer; if you started dinner, folded clothes, welcomed the children home, dropped one off at the dentist, and arbitrated numerous arguments; if you set the table between telephone calls, greeted your husband lovingly, put dinner on the table on time, cleaned the kitchen again; and if you helped with the homework, thought up ideas for science projects, made sure the children took their baths and put them to bed, went to your room, undressed, and made love to your husband—whether or not you realize it, *you are a successful woman*!

Reevaluate Time. If interruptions start interrupting interruptions, which is fairly common in my life, I know something is not right. Somehow, I have once again overextended or overcommitted myself.

Once again I have to take the time to reevaluate, to ask, is this compatible with my life's purpose? Where have I wandered from my priorities? Am I being honest and realistic about my potential and my possibilities? Have I been indiscriminate in overextending my strength and emotions? I call this self-examination *reevaluating time*. George MacDonald speaks of a "sacred idleness." He says, "Work is not always required of a man |or woman|. There is such a thing as a sacred idleness, the cultivation of which is now fearfully neglected."

God, who functions outside of our framework of time, has given us the gift of time. He foreordained a specific time for us to be a part of His eternal plan, and He has provided all of the resources, potential, and possibilities we need to accomplish all He has planned for us. If we trust Him for the wisdom and the strength to use this gift effectively and efficiently for His glory, then one day He will look at us and say, "Well done, thou good and faithful servant."

And that I call *rewarding time*, when time and eternity meet and blend.

7 Fruitful Frustration?

For twelve days it has been raining. Beside the fact that I love sunshine and tend to get depressed when the clouds hang around too long, I have had to entertain and occupy the children indoors to keep them from destroying the house and each other. On top of this, I have twenty-four fourth graders expected tomorrow for lunch and a swim, and you guessed it, the forecast is for rain—but not only for rain; a tropical storm and possible hurricane is loitering off the coast.

To say the least, I am experiencing a certain degree of frustration, and I have not been successful so far in turning this frustration into fruitfulness. Of course, this experience is not unique to me or you. As someone so aptly put it, "Mother Murphy's Law could be, A day without a crisis is a total loss." We are well acquainted with frustration. It is a part of life. We all encounter it in one way or another at some time in our lives.

WHAT IS FRUSTRATION?

Frustration, like stress, is something we all experience but that no one can really define.

One of my favorite children's books is *Alexander and the Terrible, Horrible, No Good, Very Bad Day.*[1] Alexander knows what it is to be frustrated and defeated. He says, "I went to sleep with gum in my mouth and now there's gum in my hair and when I got out of bed this morning I tripped on the skateboard and by mistake I dropped my sweater in the sink while the water was running and I could tell that it was going to be a terrible, horrible, no good, very bad day. At breakfast Anthony found the Corvette Sting Ray car kit in his cereal box . . . but in my breakfast cereal box all I found was breakfast cereal."

Alexander ends his frustrating day with, "There were lima beans for dinner and I hate limas. There was kissing on TV and I hate kissing. My bath was too hot, I got soap in my eyes, my marble went down the drain, and I had to wear my railroad-train pajamas. I hate my railroad train pajamas. When I went to bed Nick took back the pillow he said I could keep and the Mickey Mouse night light burned out and I bit my tongue. The cat wants to sleep with Anthony, not with me. It has been a terrible, horrible, no good, very bad day. My mom says some days are like that."

Alexander was experiencing many of the common, ordinary frustrations that often make up our days. Frustration is a strange mixture of negative ingredients: difficulties, stress conflicts, complications, confusion, irritation, perplexity, fatigue. And often it is the *outward circumstances beyond our control* that cause frustration. We might experience frustration when we are late for an appointment and traffic is backed up for miles because of an accident. We might encounter it again in the grocery store when the woman in the green dress pushes right in front of us in the checkout line. Perhaps we have plans to go on a long-awaited and much deserved weekend with our mate and the children come down with the flu the night before—the result: frustration.

Not long ago, all ten of us were dressed and ready for church, for once on time. Stephan and I hurried everyone out, closed and locked the door, climbed into the van, and started down the driveway. Suddenly Jerushah screamed. We turned around, only to discover that four-year-old Aram had stuck bubblegum in his little sister's long, naturally curly hair. Needless to say, I experienced a few moments of frustration as I unlocked the door and searched for the scissors.

What about the inward frustrations perhaps known only to you? Maybe you are frustrated with your physical appearance or with your personality. Perhaps you are impulsive and tend to make mistakes; you react too quickly or jump to wrong conclusions. You never seem to be dressed appropriately or always say the wrong thing.

I am often frustrated in social situations because I am very unsure of myself (I am timid by nature and so I often tend to talk too much in order to show myself friendly). I have spent years trying to learn what to say and when to say it, how not to say the wrong thing at the right time or the right thing at the wrong time, when to ask questions instead of making statements. This has caused endless hours of frustration for me.

We also often encounter frustration when a decision has to be made and we just don't know what to do. Recently, my daughter Berdjette had to make a decision concerning work, school, or a combination of both. She would look at the pros and cons of each option and make what she thought was the right decision, then the next day she would question her choice and begin all over again. She said, "Mama, I am so frustrated."

Often choices are difficult. Perhaps we lack self-confidence or things don't seem quite as simple or as black and white as they once did. Many times there are no easy solutions set before us and for some problems there *are* no solutions. We don't have answers and this causes frustration.

Perhaps your frustration is of a more serious nature. Maybe all your life you have wanted to be married and have children, but until now Mr. Right has not come into your life and you feel your plans and desires for marriage have been blocked or thwarted. Perhaps you are a single parent trying to be both breadwinner and mother. Maybe you are longing to have a child only to be disappointed month after month. Or maybe you're a young wife struggling to keep her family together or her meager budget balanced.

Although we are well aware of the presence of frustration and our responses to it, we are not sure just what frustration is, what causes it, or how to handle it in our day-to-day living. I read recently in a health supplement of a news magazine that stress, which is closely associated with frustration, arises when there is an imbalance between our perception of the demands of our lives and our belief in our ability to cope effectively.

Blocked Purposes Cause Frustration

Frustration is usually caused by conflict of one kind or another. It is closely related to defeat. For example, you are frustrated by the traffic because it will prevent you from being on time for your appointment; you are frustrated by the woman in the green dress because she usurped your right to be next in line; I was frustrated by taking my daughter back into the locked house, cutting her hair, and once again being late to church.

We encounter frustration when we are prevented from carrying out a purpose or when our intentions are blocked. We have plans for a family picnic and it rains.

Feeling Out of Control Causes Frustration

Frustration happens when we feel out of control. When we are supposed to be on top of a situation and for one reason or another we find we are not and we're prevented from accomplishing our purposes.

In *Thank You, Lord, for My Home,* I related a typical breakfast scene in our home. After ten years, the story is still very much the same and remains a favorite to many, perhaps because all can identify with it.[2]

> I awoke a little before seven, after a night of several interruptions because of the new baby in our room. I have always found it difficult to get up in the morning, a cause of frustration in itself, but usually after a cup of coffee I can begin to function. Until then, however, watch out. My family has learned, the hard way, not to expect too much from me until I have downed that coffee and even gave me a coffee mug which says, "Don't ask until I've had my coffee." On this particular morning, I arrived downstairs in anticipation of that much needed coffee only to hear a before school free-for-all in full swing going on in the kitchen. I tried to gather the strength and courage to open the kitchen door and make a dive for the coffee pot, but just as I opened the door, I saw that the two year old had spilled his orange juice. Just as I finished cleaning it up, the five year old spilled his. Before the second cleanup was completed, it was time for the four older children to leave for school. Suddenly the oldest remembered that he had not done his chores, nor had he remembered to put his gym suit in his school bag. All of a sudden, the five year old let out a powerful scream for no apparent reason, then hit the two year old. I spanked the five year old

> and consoled the two year old (still no coffee). As I tried to make my way to the coffee pot, I yelled for the oldest to "get moving." About this time the nine year old decided things were too quiet so he stirred them up by picking on one of his siblings. I scolded him and he had the nerve to argue with me. Still no coffee. Then the oldest said, "Mama, if having this many children is like this, I don't want any and why did you have so many anyway?" Hurt and terribly frustrated, I somehow managed to comb the various heads of hair, wash breakfast off their faces, pack their lunches, and usher them out the door. Once again, I turned to grab the much needed coffee when out of the corner of my eye I caught a glimpse of the two year old drinking the pancake syrup. He saw me coming and rather than relinquish his syrup, he quickly turned it upside-down, pouring it all over the carpet. I still had not had my coffee.

You may feel out of control in the battle to lose weight. You try diet after diet only to experience mounting frustration instead of melting pounds. Perhaps you had just caught up financially only to have the roof leak or the car break down. It may be that you have been working hard on a failing, unfulfilling marriage and the moment you thought things were better your husband walks out and into the arms of a younger woman. Maybe you simply can't seem to find the time and energy to complete and fulfill all your responsibilities and you stay in a constant state of frustration. You feel that life's circumstances are controlling you, and your goal each day has become simple survival. You fall into bed each night just grateful that you made it through one more day.

Small Annoyances Cause Frustration

For a woman, who is a busy mother and homemaker, especially if she also must work outside the home, the frustration of small annoyances would be more the norm than the exception. Often the simple frustrations of a busy homelife are among the most irritating.

It was the middle of summer and, like Alexander, six-year-old Stephan-Nelson was frustrated. Nothing had gone his way, and soon these small annoyances put him in a very bad mood.

He fussed and complained until I left what I was doing and went outside to be with him. We tried weeding the garden, picking apricots, taking a walk, but he continued to complain about everything. Nothing pleased him and nothing I did made him happy. Finally he looked up at me and said, "And you know, Mama, I just know that we are not going to have a good Christmas this year either. Maybe next year, but not this year."

Some days, we have every reason to feel frustrated. Often it is the small everyday annoyances that build up and cause frustration. Like cleaning the hall only to have the budding baseball star track home mud two hours later. Or discovering that it was your dog who tore up the neighbor's garbage and you have to pick it up piece by piece. Or seeing the pile of unanswered letters getting higher, or the five pounds you can't take off since vacation, or the torn wallpaper that really does need repairing. We soon feel that these small, seemingly insignificant problems have gotten the best of us.

This is often my experience. There are days when each room seems in disarray, everyone has a different schedule, everyone is in a different mood, frustrations are vented, feelings are hurt, arguments abound, children cry, teenagers tense, the telephone doesn't stop ringing, dinner burns, and I fall into bed just thankful that I am still alive.

Self-imposed Expectations Cause Frustration

Another cause of frustration is the high level of expectation we tend to place upon ourselves and others. It has been well said that "We often judge ourselves by our ideals; others, by their acts."

I have found that much of my frustration is self-precipitated and thus, avoidable. I tend to set unreasonable and often unattainable goals. I also place myself and others under the terrible burden of expectations that are not possible to reach or standards that are impossible to keep because unconsciously I am trying to fit the world's image of a successful woman. This leads to *frustrating futility*.

The great preacher Charles Spurgeon once said,

> When the game is not worth the candle, drop it. It is wasting time to look for blood in a turnip or sense in a fool. It is of no

use to hold a lantern to a mole or a looking glass to a blind man. It is not wise to aim at impossibilities—it is a waste of powder to fire at the man in the moon. It is never worthwhile to do unnecessary things. Don't make clothes for fishes or paint lilies. Never hold a candle to show the sun or try to prove a thing which nobody doubts. It is of no use ploughing the air. I would advise no one to attempt a thing which costs more than it is worth. You may sweeten a dunghill with lavender but it will turn out a losing battle in the long run.

Perfectionism Can Cause Frustration

I tend to be perfectionistic. I have often thought that is why the Lord gave me seven children; it keeps a perfectionist humble.

When I first married, I cleaned every inch of my house every day. I placed each object just as I wanted it, and if someone came in and happened to move or misplace an object, I could feel myself tense. That was before the children. Now the halo of perfectionism has drastically slipped.

Perfectionists suffer terribly from frustration. Nothing is done well enough for them so they end up doing it all themselves instead of delegating responsibility. This leads to being too busy which leads to physical exhaustion which in turn can lead to burnout and depression.

Disorganization Can Cause Frustration

However, frustration can also be the result of simple disorganization.

We look around us and everything seems piled up. The house is cluttered, there are phone calls to return, letters to answer, bills to pay, kids' clothes to buy, fingernails to polish, hair to wash—just to name a few "have-to's." Our self-esteem sinks lower and lower and we feel overwhelmed.

We need to learn to manage our time, know our own limits, and get better organized by starting with the most urgent or most dreaded thing on our list (see Chapter 6, "Where Do I Find the Time?"). We mustn't look at the forest of frustrations but must start with one tree at a time, staying with it until it is completed, then moving on to the next item until the forest becomes clearer. (It is just as frustrating to begin several projects at once, leaving many loose ends.)

Since the unexpected is bound to happen, we must also learn to flow with life's interruptions to avoid frustration. If we become either too rigid and set in our ways or too busy and overwhelmed, we are bound to experience frustration and/or burnout.

Society's Expectations Can Cause Frustration

As women, we may experience frustration as we try to adapt to the expectations of our world and society.

Conflict and Confrontation. Many of us are waking up day after day to face an environment that calls for aggressive behavior. For many this is unfamiliar territory. Women have had to learn to deal with competitive colleagues and to assert themselves more firmly. This can be somewhat frustrating for a Christian woman who feels that this type of behavior is unfeminine or unacceptable because a Christian woman is supposed to have a "gentle, quiet spirit." I experience this whenever I have to confront someone, especially if it involves a man. Each time I have to assert my authority or stand up for my rights I want to back away for fear that I will come across as tough or difficult or even hysterical, and thus lose my Christian witness.

Psychologist Gary Collins says that whenever we get frustrated we have a tendency to respond with aggression. He explains that our aggression can be of two types. Sometimes we will act overtly, lashing out with our tongues or perhaps kicking the garbage can. However, since this type of behavior is not always socially acceptable, we are more likely to react passively. Here we may smile and be charming on the outside but seethe on the inside and look for more subtle ways to express our frustration, such as by griping, gossiping, or directing our frustration and anger to another person or group.

David Augsburger addresses this problem in *Caring Enough to Confront*. He says, "Conflict is natural, normal, neutral. It can turn into painful or disastrous ends, but it doesn't need to. Conflict is neither bad nor good, right nor wrong, conflict simply is."[3]

He says that most people keep "caring" and "confronting" separate and distinct. Yet a better idea would be "care-fronting." Care-fronting, he says, calls for insight and understanding. It unifies concern for relationships with concern for goals. It is a way to communicate both impact and respect with truth and love.

Not long ago Berdjette took an expensive outfit to the cleaners. When she went to pick it up, they had lost the top. They looked for it but couldn't locate it. My daughter was patient, but after several weeks and a lot of verbal runaround from the dry cleaner, she asserted herself a little more firmly. (I would have probably let it go, fearing I would "blow it.") When she still received no response, she sweetly explained that if they didn't make the matter right by a certain date she would have no choice but to contact her lawyer. Although she held her ground, she never lost her cool. She remained in control. She was reimbursed for her loss and maintained her Christian witness.

Success. Success is another expectation that today's society often defines and measures in different terms. Success by the world's standards is often result oriented. A successful woman is one who has achieved great things or who has accomplished many things, one who makes a good salary as she balances a home and career.

This definition of success can cause a great deal of frustration for the "housewife" who is playing her part in a quiet, unassuming, supportive way. She often begins to question her self-worth if she doesn't "measure up."

I have experienced on occasion the feeling of inferiority in the presence of what many would describe as "successful women." One evening at a party I got into a conversation with a successful attorney. She was physically attractive, had a husband who was proud and supportive of her, two healthy, well-adjusted children, and her own practice. She was intelligent, articulate, successful, and feminine. As I talked with her, I must admit that although I wouldn't have traded places with her, I did feel a little inferior. I had proved that we tend to be easily influenced by what we read, see, and hear. However, the apostle Paul warned "not to let the world around you squeeze you into its own mold" (Rom. 12:2 J. B. Phillips).

Material Expectations and Discontent. Free-lance writer Susan Stevenson says, "Many of the current secular women's magazines plant seeds of *discontent*. Without realizing it, a Christian woman can find herself increasingly dissatisfied—with her husband, who is not like the men she reads about, or with herself as she notes the standards portrayed regarding physical attractiveness or self-worth."[4]

I have found this to be true in my life. I glance through the high-fashion magazines and soon realize my wardrobe doesn't even come close to these lovely creations. The gorgeous models are all thin, expertly made up, and beautifully put together. I look at *Better Homes and Gardens*. The immaculate rooms are perfectly designed and decorated and everything matches. I study the layout of plants and flowers, I look at the faultlessly manicured lawns, and then my eyes sweep my own imperfect home and yard.

How quickly the frustration of discontent can cause us to forget to be grateful and thankful! In a matter of minutes, I can become dissatisfied and discontented, longing for something I can't have.

But then I think of the woman who came to my home and said, "I love your home, it is such a friendly house." I look at that imperfect yard and think of all the children, both mine and those of the neighborhood, who enjoy building forts, digging holes, making skateboard ramps, and strewing toys everywhere, and I am grateful. I glance at myself in the mirror and thank the Lord for the healthy body that could carry and give birth to seven healthy children. I look at my closet and cringe with guilt at all of the unnecessary items hanging there—maybe they are not high fashion but I have more clothes than I need.

Timothy exhorted us, "Godliness with contentment is great gain; for we brought nothing into this world and it is certain that we can take nothing out. And having food and raiment let us be therewith content" (1 Tim. 6:6–8).

I love what C. S. Lewis said in his anthology about George McDonald, "He appears to have been a sunny, playful man, deeply appreciative of all the really beautiful and delicious things that money can buy, and no less deeply content to do without them."

Competition instead of contentment breeds frustration whether it be materially, socially, mentally, or practically. In the book of Hebrews we read, "Let your manner of life be without covetousness, and be content with such things as ye have" (Heb. 13:5). Epictetus said it well when he admonished, "Fortify yourself with contentment, for it is an impregnable fortress."

Physical

Frustration is often caused simply by our physical state.

Perhaps your frustration has its roots in physical exhaustion, a hormone imbalance, allergies, a thyroid deficiency, and so forth. So many physical problems can cause a low frustration point. If we are tired or depressed or lack energy, we experience irritation, we blow up, we lose control, and often we blame our spiritual state, when it is the physical that needs caring for.

How quickly Satan jumps on us when we are down. He loves to use our feelings as a counterfeit for faith. His calling card is discouragement and he is never more pleased with himself than when he has caused a child of God to be defeated. Understanding the ways of Satan better than I, Mother taught me many years ago that when I am down, discouraged, depressed, or defeated, I should look *first* for an answer in the physical.

A couple of years ago, I suffered from deep depression. Each morning I would open my eyes and feel a wave of depression. The tears would begin before my feet even hit the floor. I would somehow pull myself together enough to fix breakfast and get dressed. I had absolutely no energy. I went to the health food store in tears and asked for their best vitamins. I somehow managed to make it through each day but barely. I retreated from friends. I became terribly frustrated because I could no longer cope with my normal everyday responsibilities.

I tried to put up a good front, but family and friends were beginning to see that I was in bad shape. I would become angry over the smallest, most insignificant thing and then would suffer terrible guilt for having hurt those I loved best. I would feel myself losing control even in public so I didn't want to go out. I remember one day in a fast-food restaurant I waited to go to the salad bar until no one was there for fear that I would hit someone. Another time while shopping I almost lost control. I did raise my voice and begin to cry but somehow managed to leave the store without causing a scene. I no longer laughed; I had to force a smile. I felt tired and my face looked drawn. I felt I was in a hole and that each day it got a little deeper and darker. I was sure it was spiritual so I cried out to the Lord, but it was as if He had deserted me. I was desperate.

I went to one doctor who did nothing. I went to another who took a lot of blood, diagnosed me as being clinically depressed, and sent me home. I left feeling helpless and hopeless. Finally the blood tests showed I was suffering from a chemically induced depression, a result of the birth control pill I was using. Within days of changing my medication, I was free of the depression that had gripped me for nine months. Although I couldn't understand why God had allowed so many months to pass before we found the cause of my depression, it gave me real understanding and empathy for those who suffer from depression, a dark disease no one can understand unless he has experienced it himself. I became aware of our chemical makeup and that we should never underestimate it. I also saw that after periods of depression can come periods of joy and peace.

The poet William Cowper was subject to fits of depression. On one occasion he was on his way to throw himself into the River Ouse to commit suicide. He hired a coachman who purposefully lost his way thus bringing Cowper home again. The cloud of depression had left by this time and he wrote the great hymn, "God Moves in a Mysterious Way His Wonders to Perform."

Although much of the frustration we experience is normal and even unavoidable, a constant state of frustration is not normal and is not consistent with nor compatible with the fruit of the Holy Spirit. The results of constant frustration are often burnout, breakdowns, or blowups. So the important thing is not only to recognize it and understand it but to learn to deal with it. Ask yourself these questions:

Am I stretched too thin? Too overburdened? Too busy?

Am I constantly running, always behind, never "caught up"?

Am I an overachiever experiencing the "superwoman squeeze"?

Am I suffering from burnout?

DEALING WITH FRUSTRATION

Once we have recognized the fact that we do indeed experience frustration in our lives and that it is not going to go away, then we have to learn to deal with it.

First, we have to learn to pace ourselves emotionally and physically, discover our own rhythm and speed. Remember, even the tortoise made it to the finish line, and made it there first.

In *Ordering Your Private World*, Gordon MacDonald pointedly observes that we are either "called" or "driven." If you are one of those who feel "driven" by success or achievement or perfection or if you are held prisoner in the "Tyranny of the Urgent," then you are bound to encounter frustration and worse.

The Turning Point

Frustration does not always have to be negative. It can be turned into a positive force, motivating us into change and growth. Sidonie Gruenberg once said, "One of the many aspects of growing is the increasing ability to deal with frustration, to tolerate disappointment, and to draw from a thwarting experience some positive result."

Frustration can be the catalyst to change. Recently Stephan and I were in Israel. As we flew from Jerusalem to Galilee in a small plane, our guide pointed out several ponds where fish were hatched. He told us that until a few years ago the only way to feed the fish was to scatter the fish food over the entire pond. What was not eaten by the fish caused an ill-smelling layer of sediment to settle over the water. A young boy from the kibbutz was given the unpleasant job of cleaning these ponds. After several weeks, his frustration led to the discovery of a technique that released food only when the fish desired it, thus eliminating the task of cleaning the smelly ponds. This unique method is now sold worldwide.

Frustration can pressure us into working on problems we have repressed or denied. It can sometimes force us to realize that in some circumstances it is only in acceptance that we will discover peace.

So, if we aim to turn frustration into fruitfulness, then it is also vital that we be practical.

Don't Deny, Identify

First, don't deny your frustrated feelings, but begin to identify your sources of frustration. Now, this will take time. You will need some quiet time to yourself and a pad of paper. List all the things you can think of that cause you to feel frustrated—blocked goals, toddlers, a messy house, weight, job, mate, in-laws, low self-esteem, weeds, the telephone, lack of time or energy—whatever comes to your mind. Organize them into categories: personal, relational, spiritual, physical, financial, emotional. Now, for the moment, put the list aside.

Fred Smith, thinker, philosopher, businessman, says there are problems and there are "facts of life." A *problem* is something you can do something about. If you can't do anything about it, then it is *not* a problem but a *fact of life*.

While I was working on this chapter, my son Antony, age two-and-a-half, decided to turn off the word processor. This caused me to lose some material which had to be reentered. In turn, this caused me a degree of frustration. Reentering the material was frustrating because it took time I didn't have, but it was a problem that could be solved. However, Antony, age two, was simply a fact of life and he had to be accepted.

The extra thirty pounds you carry around may be frustrating, but it is a problem you can tackle. However, a physical handicap or terminal illness is a fact of life.

In other words, a problem is something you have a certain degree of control over. A fact of life, on the other hand, is a situation or a circumstance that you have little or no control over and can do nothing about, so instead of wasting precious energy in futile frustration, learn to simply accept it as a "fact of life." Remember the advice from Charles Spurgeon.

Now, look at your list. Separate the problems from the facts of life.

Facts of Life

Take your facts of life list, remembering that facts of life are the things that you have no control over and can do nothing about. With this list in front of you, get down on your knees and give them all to your heavenly Father, leaving them there with Him. After you have done this, you might already be surprised how many frustrations this simple act eliminated.

Now, the temptation will be to take them back every now and then. It is often easier to work on and tackle our problems than it is to entrust our facts of life to God. If you find yourself once again under the frustrating burden of carrying them around, go back to your knees.

Problems

Now, take the problems list. This list you will keep close at hand because you will be adding and crossing items off periodically.

First of all, look at it closely.

Be honest. Why do these things frustrate you? For example, if you have listed a messy house, does it frustrate you because you don't have the time to clean, or because it attacks your pride to have your friends see a less than perfect home? Is it laziness? Would you rather shop and watch the soaps? Is your frustration lack of time? Do you waste time? Are you disorganized? If you used your time wisely, could you find a bit more? Be honest.

Then, put your problems in *perspective*. Will they still frustrate you in five years? Fifty years? If you are objective, can you say, "This too will pass"? Perhaps you have several small children. They will grow and before you know it, they will be on their own, leaving you with a spotless house but an empty place in your heart. Stephan and I just drove our third child, Basyle, to college. At home I walk down the hallway and see the room I so often reminded him to clean. It is spotless now but empty.

In perspective, is there happiness in your home? Which is more important, a happy home or an immaculate one? The fingerprints on the window or the little hands that made them? After my children had spent a few weeks once with my mother, she told her housekeeper to leave the fingerprints on the windows as a happy memory. That's frustration in perspective.

Another time I was working on this chapter, the telephone rang. It was Stephan informing me that two children of very close friends had been in an accident. He asked if I could go with him to the hospital to see them. As I was getting ready to leave, Aram, ten, arrived home from school and told me he had fallen and torn his new school pants. Ordinarily I would have scolded him for not being more careful but because of the phone call, I quickly put this problem in perspective. I sweetly told him I was sorry but just so grateful he wasn't hurt.

Often life is like using a camera. When we focus in on the more important problems, the others tend to blur. But if we try to focus on the entire picture of problems, nothing is clear. Thus, constant frustration.

I have picked simple examples, and I am very aware that many of you experience frustrations that are much more complex than these. But the principles remain the same. Whatever the frustration, put it in perspective. Step back and look at it again. Ask honest questions and especially ask, how does this look from the perspective of eternity?

A *positive attitude* helps keep frustrations in perspective. Negative thinking leads to negative reactions and then to negative actions. I personally believe that being negative is a habit. It just encourages and emphasizes frustration. The rewards of breaking the habit are less frustrating situations and a more pleasant environment for all. I know, because the negative habit is one that I have been aware of in my own life.

As Bob Schuller says, "Eliminate the negative by accentuating the positive."

H*umor* helps keep life in perspective. It is a great lubricator and antidote to frustration. Learn to see the ridiculous. Laugh at yourself and look for the humorous side to even difficult situations. Remember that the same God who created us with the ability to shed tears also enabled us to find relief through laughter.

My maternal grandfather, Dr. Nelson Bell, had a winning way of using humor to ease tension. If my grandmother lost her patience or snapped at him occasionally, he would good-naturedly laugh or tease her. He was hard of hearing and often when she called him to dinner, he couldn't hear. She would call again. No answer. Again she called loudly enough for him to hear and to realize that her patience was near the limit. He would arrive in the dining room with a twinkle in his eye visibly shaking from head to toe. Then he would suddenly jump up and crack his heels together, making her laugh and forget her impatience.

One of our friends has a family saying, "Laugh or have high blood pressure." They laugh.

Now, *prioritize* your list.

Which frustrations are the most irksome? Start working on the first one and keep going. You may have to be willing to make some changes and this might take courage. A friend of mine with a husband and three children was very active in all manner of activities. The junior league, church, school, neighborhood, you name it and she was or had been or soon would be involved. Suddenly she realized what all of this was doing to herself and to her family so she began to say no. This took courage, but she is reaping the benefits of a healthy body and a happy home.

Be patient, positive, and persistent. Begin to tackle your frustrating problems, but do not expect overnight results or immediate victories. Some problems may take years to solve. My house will not be spic and span until my children are all grown. Considering that the youngest is two, I have a long wait and by then there will be grandchildren. So once again, I just "Praise and Pray and Peg away."

Be patient. Be content with even the smallest result.

Be positive. If results seem small and changes slow, don't be negative. Look for the positive side of each problem you are tackling and be positive about the way you are tackling it. At least you can give yourself an "A" for trying.

Be persistent. Don't give up. Don't be discouraged if and when you fail. Remember, discouragement is the devil's calling card.

After all this work there will still be many days and certain situations when we have done all we know to do and yet we remain in a state of confusion and frustration. Like Alexander's mother said, "Some days are like that." But then we go a step farther. Like we did with the "facts of life," we get down on our knees and give it all to our heavenly Father. Then we sit and watch His power work and His plan unfold.

King Jehoshaphat had just such an experience (see 2 Chron. 20). Although he had a vast army, his enemies had formed an alliance and had "come against Jehoshaphat to battle." He was surrounded on every side and "Jehoshaphat feared." He was frustrated. His plans had been thwarted, his purposes blocked, and he had lost control of the situation. He knew the whole nation was looking to him for directions and answers but he had none. He was both inwardly and outwardly frustrated. He was physically and emotionally exhausted.

But Jehoshaphat was a godly man and so he "set himself to seek the Lord." He fasted and prayed, "We have no might against this great company that cometh against us; neither know we what to do: but our eyes are upon thee." Then Jehoshaphat waited and trusted.

The Lord answered, "Be not afraid nor dismayed by reason of this great multitude [of frustration]. The battle is not yours, but God's. Ye shall not need to fight, set yourselves, stand still, and see the salvation of the Lord."

Before the battle was won, Jehoshaphat began to praise the Lord because He was fighting and winning the battle for Israel. And the "spoil," or fruitfulness, was so great that it took Jehoshaphat and his men three days to gather it.

For many years Stephan and I lived in Switzerland. Once we were looking for a new home, and I began to pray very specifically not only for a home but for certain things I wished for in the home—a fireplace, a stream in the yard, a view (preferably of Les Dents du Midi, my favorite mountain whose three peaks came to represent for me the Trinity), at least four bedrooms, preferably five.

Stephan looked over my petition and informed me that our budget could not afford such a home. But to Stephan's surprise the Lord did give us just such a home, down to the last detail (even the favorite mountain peak). We were thrilled and soon we were settled in and life seemed as sure and serene as the snow-covered mountains around us.

Then one night, I awoke to noise. I looked out the window to see strange men wandering around our yard. I opened our bedroom door on the second floor and saw water rushing toward me. I quickly woke Stephan, grabbed my Bible and a few pieces of jewelry, rushed to gather the children, and fled. By a freak accident, our home had been flooded, and the firemen were there to evict us for fear of a landslide. So we left our little house and all of our possessions and moved into what we thought was a temporary arrangement. However, soon afterward, Stephan was drafted into the army and I was left alone with the children in unpleasant, uncomfortable, and very frustrating circumstances, with Christmas just around the corner.

I was confused. Why had God allowed this? First my prayers were so beautifully answered, then so suddenly my idyllic situation was exchanged for a very frustrating, confining one. It was cold and damp and the children got sick. Soon I became ill, too. I dreaded each day. I could no longer see Les Dents du Midi. It was often hard to feel the presence of God.

Then my mother wrote the following poem for me:

Above the clouds
thick, boiling, low,
appear the peaks
she came to know
as Father, Son
and Holy Ghost;
often when she
sought them most
they would be hid
in clouds from view.
Distraught by cares
she always knew,
silent, unseen,
they still were there,
like God Himself—
unchanged, serene;
knowing this
she gathered strength
for each day's journey—
length by length.
Ruth Bell Graham

Unseen and unknown to me, God was at work. He was exercising and tightening spiritual muscles I never knew I had and would never have discovered if I hadn't been placed in a situation where I was forced to use them. Although I was uncomfortable and frustrated, God was using these very circumstances to shape and mold and build me up spiritually.

There was an old, worn red velvet chair in my room and because of my frustration and desperation, I began to spend much of my time curled up in that chair with the Lord. Soon I began to fix my eyes upon Him instead of my frustrating circumstances. And it wasn't long before I discovered with David that in the midst of frustrating circumstances "He had enlarged my heart" (see Ps. 119:32). I began to see my priorities and motives and value in light of His Word. I began to look beyond the horizon of my frustration and see that God was bringing fruitfulness out of my frustration.

Often the confinement of difficulties causes frustration. But given to God, these very frustrating elements can bring growth. Knowing my frustration, Mother once shared with me a story told by Reverend Crate Jones of Durham, North Carolina.

> On the edge of Louisville, Kentucky, runs a canal, containing a set of locks through which ships must pass to move from a lower level of the Ohio River to a higher one.
>
> I watched a ship enter the first set of locks one day. First, the giant front gates closed; then the rear gates, rendering the huge ship immobile.
>
> To the casual observer, nothing seemed to be happening. But underneath, the intake valves were opening to allow the water to flood the chamber. Gradually the ship rose to the next water level. Then the gates were opened and the ship moved easily into the next set of locks. The process was repeated until the ship was able to continue its journey on the upper level of the Ohio.
>
> This is a parable of life. There are times when we are locked in—through illness, disappointment, failure, or trouble wearing one of its many garbs. Being unable to move either forward or backward, we are forced to wait. But something is happening whether we realize it or not. Beneath us God has opened the valve of His love, and His mighty power is at work. He is lifting us!

Presently the gates open, and we move out on a higher level. We discover that our confidence in God to work all things for our good (Rom. 8:28) has risen to a new high. Depending on the complexity of our problem, the process may have to be repeated several times. Each time we rise a little higher. In the midst of it all, the Spirit whispers to our hearts, "The eternal God is your refuge, and underneath are the everlasting arms" (Deut. 33:27).

In those hemmed-in times we hear God say, "Be still, and know that I am God" (Ps. 46:10). There we learn to trust Him and dare to believe our troubles are not here to stay, but that they will pass.

Ships are meant for sailing, not for remaining closed in the high places in God's plan. We may go through the locks, but we won't be stranded there. Life is a series of locks, and the last ones through which we will pass will find us docking at the port of heaven! What comfort and encouragement this illustration gave me.

Locks take many shapes and forms, and everyone experiences them at some time—an unhappy marriage, a boring job, illness, loneliness, finances. Whatever the particular situation, I have discovered through the years, that what we often perceive as sorrows, trials, stress, or restraints of one kind or another may actually be hidden blessings.

There have been many frustrating "locks" in my life. Difficulties, loneliness, misunderstandings, small annoyances. Many times I have questioned "Why?" when I felt confined and hemmed in by circumstances. But I discovered that if I am to turn these frustrations into fruitfulness, the question is not so much "Why?" as it is "To what end?" There will always be times we don't know why. There may even be times when the purpose is hidden. It is then that we must walk in faith, believing in a loving heavenly Father.

I love the quote by James Renwick, the seventeenth-century Scottish Covenanter: "Faith can read love in God's heart when His face frowns." It is often through life's frustrations that we once again discover the great truth of fruitfulness, that when Jesus is all we have, He is all we really need.

Do you remember that day I was expecting twenty-four kids for a swim party? Well, we prayed and during the night, the storm went back out to sea. By lunchtime, the sky had cleared, the sun was out, and twenty-four children had a wonderful party.

Clad in blue jeans and a T-shirt, I was serving up hot dogs and beans when one little boy looked up into my face and said, "You're pretty."

The last of my frustration disappeared along with his shy smile. My caring, loving heavenly Father was concerned about helping me turn my frustration into fruitfulness.

Of course, all frustrating problems are not solved so easily, but often our loving Lord gives us just enough encouragement so that we can go on.

"Let us run with patience the race that is set before us" (Heb. 12:1b).

8 *Weed and Feed?*

We have a rather large yard for southern Florida and, since we have a twelve-month growing season, we seem to spend numerous hours working in it. My sons often balk at another Saturday doing yard work, so I repeatedly point out to them that "subduing the land" existed before the Fall and was considered a privilege for Adam. Even this biblical encouragement doesn't seem to have much effect on their attitudes.

One day as were were "subduing" vines and leaves, Aram, whose job it was to pick up leaves, just kept plopping from leaf pile to leaf pile all the while singing at the top of his eight-year-old lungs, "Work, work, I hate work. It's so dumb and dull."

I have to admit, I thought he had a point, but someone has to do it. Twice a year, we have to fertilize our lawn. We usually choose Weed and Feed which is supposed to kill the weeds and feed the grass. However, we always do this with fear and trepidation, since the weeds outnumber the grass. What if we awaken one morning to a dead yard?

One year as we were repeating the weeding and feeding process, I wondered, *Isn't this what the Holy Spirit is supposed to do in our lives?* When we become Christians, the Holy Spirit weeds out the unhealthy, unwholesome, negative desires that influence us and replaces them with wholesome desires for spiritual, mental, and moral well-being. Paul said, "If any man be in Christ he is a new creature: old things are passed away, behold all things are become new" (2 Cor. 5:17). And in Hebrews, God said, "I will put My laws into their hearts, and in their minds I will write them" (Heb. 10:16).

EXPOSURE

A few months ago, I went to the dermatologist with one of my sons. During the visit, I asked the doctor about some of the new techniques used to remove wrinkles (I am at the age where this is of great interest). He explained a few of the techniques to me and then handed me a brochure concerning the dangers of exposure to the sun's harmful rays.

"White is in," he declared dogmatically. This was hard for me to accept since I love the look of suntanned skin and I live in sunny Florida where it is possible to have a tan all year.

We are quite frequently warned about the dangers of certain exposures: cigarette smoke, drugs, dyes, preservatives, and chemicals. We are required to vaccinate ourselves against exposure to germs and diseases. Recently we have even been made aware of certain communities that are dangerous because of exposure to radiation. A rock singer was sued recently because it was suspected that exposure to the lyrics of his songs may have caused at least one young teenager to take his own life.

What we permit our minds and bodies to be exposed to is extremely important. This is especially true for Christians because we are taught in Scripture that we no longer belong to ourselves. The apostle Paul had this reminder for the early Christians: "What? know ye not that your body is the temple of the Holy Ghost which is in you, which ye have of God, and ye are not your own? For ye are bought with a price: therefore glorify God in your body, and in your spirit, which are God's" (1 Cor. 6:19–20, KJV).

Many Christians don't realize how much they indulge in mental "junk food"—immoral movies; dull-witted, unintelligent television programs; poorly written books; cheap magazines; inferior music. We are becoming so accustomed to the mediocre and inferior that we not only accept it, we actually begin to enjoy it.

The first season a certain nighttime soap was aired on television, I got hooked. Each week I hurried to get the youngest children in bed and at nine o'clock I sat down in front of the TV. No one could say a word. Mother could not be disturbed. Stephan just went to bed an hour earlier or he and the boys went to talk in the kitchen.

At first, I was a bit shocked and disgusted by the immoral actions and attitudes of the characters; then, after a few weeks I began to accept the portrayal of evil even though I never felt comfortable with it. Gradually it dawned on me that I was spending hours watching a program that portrayed divorce, incest, homosexuality, adultery, and decadence. I was slowly becoming desensitized to the horror and loathsomeness of these sins. Suddenly I realized I was exposing myself to an influence that not only portrayed but glamorized the sins my Savior died to deliver men and women from. I remembered the verse, "Ye that love the Lord, hate evil" (Ps. 97:10 KJV). So I quit watching.

A good verse to tape on top of our television sets to remind us to be aware of what we are watching is, "I will set no wicked thing before mine eyes" (Ps. 101:3 KJV).

Now, please do not misunderstand me. I am not necessarily discussing "Christian" versus secular; I am discussing good versus bad, although often the two go hand-in-hand. Books do not necessarily have to be Christian or religious in nature to be good. There is much written today that is worthy reading not to mention all the classics. Music doesn't have to be "religious" to have beauty and quality. There are many superior films on television and in the theaters that are well worth the viewing time, even though some Christians consider these films secular in nature.

Some people tend to think that only religious art forms can be "good." Edith Schaeffer said in *Common Sense Christian Living*, that people are apt to forget that God made human beings in the first place. The music (or writing or film) that pours forth could never do so had He not made such amazing creatures as human beings with their diversity of talents.

Mrs. Schaeffer further says that paintings, films, music, interior decorating do not have to be "religious" to be Christian. We can appreciate all these gifts with hearts full of praise to God. Praise Him and stand in awe of such great diversity. We are not to have a narrow, limited view of our God, nor are we to have a narrow, limited view of what He provides for us to enjoy. The fact is, He "gives us richly all things to enjoy" (1 Tim. 6:17).

As we were saying (before I got sidetracked), the Holy Spirit is working within us to change our tastes and desires. However, Satan is also at work making his evil ideas and lifestyles more available and more attractive. We must use discernment to decide which are harmful. This is accomplished as we actively cooperate with the Holy Spirit in the whole process of "weeding and feeding." How do we do this? We begin by weeding and feeding the basic areas of our lives.

WEED AND FEED PERSONALLY AND SOCIALLY

First, take a look at your life. Look at your day. How do you spend it? Are you productive, or do you waste many hours? Now, I am not talking about hours spent resting or relaxing. These are very needed hours. I'm talking about hours that are truly wasted. When you look back on your day, are you pleased with the way you used the time God gave you? Or are you using precious moments to cultivate weeds?

Recognize the Weeds

Our children are not allowed candies and chocolate except on Sunday and special days like birthdays. Not long ago, two-year-old Antony was discovered with a mouthful of chocolate. I strongly reprimanded him and reminded him that he was only allowed candy on Sunday. He nodded his little head in acknowledgment and then after he swallowed the offending delight, he said, "I will just go to the refrigerator and open the door and say hi to the chocolate."

Each one of us is tempted by things that fertilize weeds. Your temptation might not be mine. I am not tempted often by chocolate nor do I like daytime TV. I find it boring and a terrible waste of time, but I have friends who are really addicted to certain soaps. On the other hand, delicious bread and hot muffins and sale racks attract me like a magnet. I could easily be tempted to "bargain hunt" several times a week just for fun. Perhaps you spend too many hours talking on the phone, participating in a sport, or even cleaning your house. Perhaps you are addicted to trashy novels or gossip. Learn to recognize the weeds in your life.

The temptations to *procrastinate* or *avoid* a given responsibility are often weeds that choke our time. We would rather put it off or try to avoid it altogether than just begin it and get it done. Henry Ford once said that "Most people spend more time and energy going around problems than trying to solve them."

One day when Basyle, our eighteen-year-old son and chief lawn mower, was younger, I noticed that the mowed grass had a peculiar pattern to it, not straight lines, but a sort of weaving back and forth. Mother, who was visiting, and I were sitting out on our back terrace while Basyle was mowing. After a while, she, too, became curious about the funny pattern in the grass so she went to investigate. She laughingly called me to come survey the cause. Each time Basyle came upon an obstacle, a rock, a large stick, a toy, he just went around it, thus avoiding it altogether rather than getting off the tractor and taking the time to remove it. We called his attention to the strange pattern and advised him that such a job was unacceptable.

Procrastination is a waste of time, since unsolved problems and undone chores leave strange patterns in our daily lives just like improperly mowed grass. Procrastination simply leaves an undone burden hanging over our heads. I tend to find this weed when facing my correspondence and certain areas of housekeeping (like closets and drawers).

Weeding and feeding also means recognizing those things in our lives that may not necessarily be "bad" in themselves but rob us of valuable "feeding" time we need for cultivating and nourishing our minds and spirits. For example, being too busy is the most persistent weed in my garden. I clear my calendar only to find it suddenly filled again. It is a weed that has to be pulled almost daily.

Take inventory. Where could you pull a few weeds so that there would be more time for feeding? Another example: when I write a book, my editor tightens up my manuscript. He or she takes an objective look at my work, and then changes a word here or takes out a sentence there in order to simplify and clarify the book, making it less cluttered and thus more interesting and effective. This is what I mean by "weeding." Take a look at your days. Tighten up, simplify your schedule, or clear out some clutter so that you have more time available for "feeding," thus making your life more interesting and effective.

Weed Bad Habits

Be aware of *habits*. Some people flip on the television or radio as soon as they get out of bed in the morning and keep it on all day. Have you ever gotten into someone's car and found the radio already on? You carry on a conversation (or try to) above the din of some music or commentaries which neither you nor the other person is really listening to. The radio is just on out of habit. Do you ever find yourself flipping on the TV out of habit? While there is nothing wrong with television in moderation, we often fill our minds with trash just because we are not disciplined enough to turn the set off.

Someone once said that the chains of habit are generally too small to be felt until they are too strong to be broken. Those who spend endless hours watching soaps or game shows might decide to fill that time by reading a good book therefore avoiding the temptation to turn on the television. I know that when I am dieting, I try to be busy during my normal lunch time so that I don't think of food.

Mark Twain once said, "A habit cannot be tossed out the window, it must be coaxed down the stairs a step at a time." I have found that replacing a habit with another activity helps to break it.

Weed Relationships

Friendships play a vital role in the weeding and feeding process. Do you have "friends" who feed the weeds in your life? Perhaps they take up hours of your valuable time unnecessarily. Or perhaps you are involved in a relationship that is unhealthy or even sinful. You may have to trim these friendships or even avoid some of them altogether.

My friend's marriage was at a precarious point. I tried to encourage her to do all she could to save her marriage. She and her husband were both Christians and there was no third party involved. However, she chose to spend much of her time with certain friends from the country club who were recently divorced. They encouraged her to

"Go ahead, get divorced"; "It's not the end of the world"; "You can make it on your own." She listened to these "friends" and soon she divorced her husband and added her three children to the rising numbers who are from broken homes.

In the Old Testament we find harsh treatment ordered against friends or even relatives who enticed the children of Israel away from the Lord (see Deut. 13:6–9). Although we Christians today would not carry out this same punishment, God has placed this verse in Scripture to show us the seriousness of friendships.

Others in your life drain you emotionally, physically, or spiritually. They rob you of many valuable hours unnecessarily. Some people demand an unfair amount of attention as if it is their "right" like the bumper sticker that reads, "I was born entitled." Others like to gossip or just talk about trivia for hours. They unburden all their problems on you, which makes them feel great afterward but you feel like the garbage disposal. Some people are just not good for you as their influence is continually fighting the "new life" that the Holy Spirit is cultivating.

I once had a friend who discovered her husband was involved with another woman. She was understandably crushed. Every day, sometimes twice a day, for weeks, she would call me and talk for several hours going over the situation again and again, rehashing each detail. I felt exhausted and drained after each phone call, and we accomplished little. I was pouring valuable energy and countless hours into this friend, yet she remained the same day after day whereas I was depleted and empty.

Now, I am not saying we are to avoid those friends and acquaintances to whom we are ministering and witnessing. But I am saying we are to be cautious about how we use our time and energies.

Not long ago eight-year-old Jerushah came home from school and I asked her how she was.

"A little tired," she replied.

"Why?" I asked.

"Well," she explained, "I had a bad day."

"Tell me about it," I encouraged.

"Well," she began, "everyone got into a fight except me and two other girls, so everyone came to me to solve their problems. I helped a few, then they all came. I got so tired trying to help them all that I said to myself, 'I wish I had never helped the first one.'"

John Sanford, in his book *Ministry Burnout*, said, "The energy drain that comes from working with people in need is subtle. . . . It's like having a small but constant loss of blood." When a layperson tries to counsel without the proper tools, many valuable hours can be wasted, and he can quickly find himself burned out.

We need to seek out and cultivate those friendships that bring out the best in us. I am sure you have spent time with someone and afterward felt refreshed, stimulated, and motivated. You were a better person for having been with that friend. My friend Lorraine is always a blessing to be with. She encourages me in the Lord, uplifts me, and reminds me that the Lord's strength is sufficient. She never gossips, is always positive, and holds me to my highest.

A friend who is a new believer in Christ recently moved into a new neighborhood where there are several Christians. One day she told me she was certain God had placed her and her husband in their new environment so they could develop a new set of friends.

Friends play such an important role in our Christian growth.

WEED AND FEED INTELLECTUALLY: DEVELOP AND NURTURE NEW TASTES

When I married Stephan and moved to Europe, there were many foods I had never seen much less tried before. One of these was the artichoke. I remember the first time his family served me one. They placed before me a large, rather odd, greenish-brown object that was most unappetizing and almost frightening in appearance. I thought I was being served a large cooked pinecone. The first bite was the most difficult, and the consecutive bites were not much better. However, after this delicacy had been placed before me on several different occasions, I found myself tolerating it, then enjoying it, and now I often crave an artichoke.

New tastes can be developed and nourished. Often, simple exposure causes tastes to change. Just as negative exposure to "weeds" can be ruinous, positive exposure can be beneficial. As the television commercial used to say, "Try it, you'll like it." If you like trashy novels or mediocre music, you can develop a taste for classical concerts, biographies, or historical novels.

When I was young, I thought all classical music was "long-haired," old-fashioned, and just plain dreadful. It even left my nerves bare, especially the violin, which I thought shrieked. I had not had much exposure to classical music as a child, but when I married and moved to Europe where so many of the great composers lived and wrote their masterful works, I developed a great appreciation for classical music. I found myself appreciating the clear, true clarinets and flutes, the power-filled organs, the magnificent brass, the delicate strings. I even grew to appreciate the highly polished instruments themselves and the men and women God had gifted to render their majestic sounds. And of course I admired those who were inspired to write the music.

You can discipline yourself to develop your tastes for the good, the mind-rewarding, the character-building, the pure. Scripture gives us guidelines in this area: "Whatever things are true, whatever things are honest, whatever things are just, whatever things are pure, whatever things are lovely, whatever things are of good report; if there be any virtue, and if there be any praise, think on these things" (Phil. 4:8).

Nourish Your Desires

Most of us have secret desires especially in my age group and older. Many of us never finished our educations. Most of us didn't have the choices and options that younger women have today, and we look at them a little enviously because we carry a secret desire in our heart. Once the children are grown or are in school all day, we may be able to fill some of the empty hours by developing our secret desires. If we are not careful, weeds will try to sprout at this time. We may head for the mall or spend more hours in front of the television. And if we are not careful our minds will begin to vegetate and our bodies begin to sag.

This is the time to develop your secret desire. You have always wanted to finish your education; do it. You have always had a desire to learn a foreign language; do it. You have always wanted to learn to paint, sew, wallpaper, decorate cakes, take an aerobics class; do it. One of my regrets in life is not learning Hebrew when I lived in Israel. My husband took courses in Hebrew, and I had someone available to care for my infant son, but I was too timid; so I found numerous excuses not to take advantage of this unique opportunity. Now I regret it.

Most local colleges offer interesting opportunities for women who wish to go back to school. Many even offer credits for what they call "life experience." Local community centers list a variety of courses in crafts, languages, arts. Fabric and craft stores have a wide range of classes, too.

Remember the turtle: he only makes progress when he sticks his neck out.

I had a friend who began to take organ lessons when her youngest child decided to take piano lessons. Another friend went back to college with her daughter and they received their R.N. degrees together. Still another friend got her law degree, passed the bar, and now has her own private practice. None of these women is extraordinary. They had a secret desire, and slowly, persistently, one step at a time, while their friends wasted away their days, they nurtured their secret goals. They dared to develop their desires.

I have another friend who also has a secret desire to finish college. She even seems a bit resentful sometimes that she has been denied her education. Although she has the time and resources available to her, she only talks about her desire. I know others who are gifted or talented in certain areas and allow their gifts to go to waste because they are lazy or procrastinators or avoiders. They waste valuable time dealing with weeds instead of cultivating their gardens of usefulness.

I am often asked how I began to write. I do not consider myself a professional writer since I was never trained as a writer. But it was my secret desire. In fact, just a few weeks ago, Luverne Gustavson, who was my daddy's secretary when I was a young girl, reminded me that when I was fourteen I told her one day I would like to write a book on raising children.

When the opportunity came I took it although I was terribly afraid. I figured there are fifty-two weeks in a year. If I only wrote one page a week, I could write a book in three years. My time was very limited, but I knew that with a certain amount of discipline, I could develop my desire a little bit at a time. First Timothy 6:17 said God has given us richly *all* things to enjoy, and I believed that includes all the opportunities that become available to us.

Be Informed—In Case . . .

Being informed means knowing specific details of the family finances. If not, we may be in the same situation as Becky Barker, an attractive young wife and mother of two small daughters, who suddenly lost her husband in an automobile accident. The initial shock was very difficult to deal with, but from the first day another shock wave hit as she discovered just how ignorant she was about the family finances.

"Do you have insurance?"

"I don't know," she replied.

"How many bank accounts do you have?"

"I don't know."

"Where is the key to your husband's safe deposit box?"

Again her answer was, "I don't know."

"Do you know the name of someone who does have this information?"

"No."

Becky was forced to spend days searching for this information until she became an emotional wreck. Along with her sister Suzi, Becky wrote a book called *Answers*, which gives women the practical advice they need to avoid just such a situation as she suffered. (For a copy of the book *Answers*, write Answers, Inc., Dept. BH, P.O. Box 72666 Corpus Christi, Texas 78472.)

Some statistics point out that the average age of a widow is fifty-two and that eleven out of twelve women will be widowed. How important it is for us to be informed and involved with the family finances!

Last year, I decided to increase my limited knowledge in this area. I vaguely knew where the important papers were and the name of our lawyer and insurance agent, but I had little understanding of how to keep accounts, balance a checkbook, discuss insurance needs, get a loan, sell a house, or make investments. So I enrolled in a course at our local college entitled, "Personal Finance," which was among the wisest decisions I have ever made. I now have a working knowledge of family and personal finance. I am more informed which gives me more confidence. I now feel comfortable when the bank calls or the insurance agent wants to review our insurance needs.

FEED THROUGH CONVERSATION AND READING

When Stephan-Nelson was a little fellow, his younger sister, Berdjette, looked at him and said, "Tetan doesn't have any brains, he just has a head."

I am often concerned when I listen to my children. They live in a visual generation. They don't enjoy reading books that take concentration of thought or wrestling with a problem. They have a difficult time thinking a problem through and working it out regardless of whether it's a scholastic, social, or even practical problem since they're used to seeing the solution of all problems, no matter how complex, in half-hour segments on television. They cringe when I suggest that they watch the film series *Marco Polo*. "Oh mother," they moan, "how boring!" What they mean by this is that they might have to use a few more little gray cells than if they watched reruns of "Leave it to Beaver" or the cartoons.

Unfortunately, mental laziness is evident. Many people seem to have a sign over their heads which reads, "Don't Feed the Brain."

I was just out of high school when I married Stephan and moved to Europe. Although I was a good thinker I had not often practiced the art of reflection or been exposed to the process of logical thinking.

In Europe conversation is an enjoyable pastime. Europeans love to philosophize and moralize and spend many hours in thoughtful debate. I would often sit for hours in a formal drawing room of a gracious home on Lake Geneva or outside in the garden under the shade of a large umbrella listening to these deep discussions, which usually were theological or political in nature. Long after we had all enjoyed numerous cups of tea and debated just as many ideas and thoughts, I would watch the sun sink lower and lower in the sky and see shadows creep slowly across the lawn. When we could no longer see one another, a few lights would be turned on, more tea would be served, and the discussion would continue. Suddenly, for no apparent reason other than the lateness of the hour, the conversation would come to an abrupt end for this American teenage activist. Since nothing had been accomplished, I considered these afternoons quite a shameful waste of time.

Years later I realized the value of these many hours of listening. I had begun to learn the art of pondering a problem or a subject, discussing it, and debating it until I had come to some solid conclusions. Strength is often related to the ability to think and analyze. I discovered the value of good, meaningful thought and analysis.

Somerset Maugham once said that "Conversation is one of the greatest pleasures in life, but it wants leisure." Stephan and I still prefer good conversation to any other form of relaxation. We often spend the evening talking with friends or we go to a small restaurant, and just talk between ourselves. I often find this time so stimulating that I have difficulty sleeping afterward.

In the book of Proverbs we read, "A friendly discussion is as stimulating as the sparks that fly when iron strikes iron" (Prov. 27:17 TLB). Just as it is important to have friends you can really relax with, it is important to develop friendships that stimulate your mind. But in order to have meaningful conversations, you have to have something to talk about. Again weeding and feeding is important.

Keep informed. Read the newspaper or watch the news at least once a day. Be aware of what is going on in the world. Read at least one weekly news magazine a week. One of the nicest gifts my mother gave me was a globe. It's nice to know where the places discussed in the news are located. Finding them on the globe is educational for the whole family.

Stay abreast of the best seller list. Even though you may not wish to read all these books yourself, being aware of what others are reading is important.

I never finished college, and this fact has often caused me to feel inferior intellectually. Because of this lack, I often take advantage of opportunities to increase my knowledge and sharpen my mind. When Stephan decided to return to school in order to earn his Ph.D., I took a few courses too, which gave us extra time together, stimulated my mind, and advanced my own goal of one day completing my degree.

Reading is one of the best, easiest, and most accessible means of mind stimulation. For this reason, I review books for a Christian book-club. This forces me to read at least one book a month that is being offered in the Christian market. I enjoy reading and have taught myself to speed read and skim books that I may not wish to read word for word.

A good rule of thumb: for every ten new books you read, read a classic. Reading these masterpieces disciplines your mind and exposes you to good literature as well as a beautiful use of the English language that is all but lost today.

Someone once said, "A classic is a book that has never finished saying what it has to say." But the word *classic* frightens many people. Each summer, I have my children read three books: one spiritual, one of their choice, and one classic. You should hear the complaints about the "classic" choice.

We don't need to be intimidated by classics. Classics come in all shapes and sizes and don't have to be limited to Victor Hugo (I would rather watch *Les Miserables* on TV, too) or *David Copperfield* or even Shakespeare if his works are not to your taste. I suggest classics like *Tom Sawyer, Little Lord Fauntleroy, The Little Princess, Kidnapped, The Cloister and the Hearth, Lorna Doone*, just to name a few exciting ones. My family also enjoys *Winnie the Pooh, The Secret Garden, The Chronicles of Narnia*, and *The Hobbit*.

Erudition and Entertainment

Historical novels and biographies are a wonderful and stimulating way to learn history. I know little of the twelfth century so recently I read Louis L'Amour's *The Walking Drum*. I was amazed at all I learned while thoroughly enjoying myself. I learned something of Russian history reading a biography of Tolstoy's wife, *Sonya*, as well as *Nicholas and Alexandria*, by Robert Massie. Books by authors like James Michener who heavily research their chosen subject are an excellent source of erudition plus entertainment.

Read magazines and periodicals. Read at least one or two Christians periodicals as well as a national women's magazine a month. *The National Geographic* is an excellent source of information, as well as superb visual stimulation. Month after month our family is carried away to the far corners of the world.

Discipline yourself to read, or at least thumb through, books, journals, or magazine articles having to do with subjects that naturally *do not* interest you. This broadens and stretches your mind, and you might be surprised to discover that a simple child's science book might spark an interest in the field of science. Reading my son's *Popular Mechanics* has made me want to know more about my car (I haven't had time to learn how to change sparkplugs or oil but would like to). *Money Magazine* has opened my mind to the world of finance. Since Stephan is a psychologist and my interests don't fall in this area, I try to read psychological journals or books relating to the subject. This increases my knowledge of his field of interest, he has more respect for my opinion, and he often asks my advice.

Allow Your Situation to Stimulate Your Knowledge

Often we fight our situations when we should allow them to stimulate our knowledge. In the early years of our marriage, Stephan and I moved a great deal. We moved from Switzerland to Israel, back to Switzerland, and then to France—more than twelve times in ten years. At first I grumbled and complained. Then I realized I had a unique opportunity to learn. I tried to learn something about the history, the culture, the customs, the habits, and the people in each place we lived. Just sitting in a local café drinking a Coke and watching people was a learning experience, and in looking back, I wouldn't trade those stretching experiences for anything.

Recently Berdjette took a job in Washington, D.C. She had never been too interested in politics or American history, but her interest was sparked when she began to live in our nation's capital.

When my friend Bette first got married, she took a year off from teaching to travel with her husband whose job took him to various cities around the country. She had never before been "unemployed," and having a whole "free" day in a motel room in a strange city, "scared me until I came up with my 'sanity-saver city plan.' In every major city and town we hit, I immediately canvassed the churches, volunteered my time, checked special events in town, visited sight-seeing spots, scoured the library, perused museums and shopping malls, and met as many local people as possible by attending church services including Sunday school. I found this tremendously broadening."

And for those of you who have never lived anywhere but your hometown: do you know its history? What about the wildlife? The people? My hometown, Asheville, North Carolina, seemed dull to me until I discovered all sorts of interesting facts about it. Thomas Wolfe called it home. Scott Fitzgerald also spent time there after his wife Zelda suffered a mental breakdown and was placed in the local mental hospital (rumors say she died in a fire that destroyed the top floor of the hospital). Walt Disney worked for a while in Asheville, and as a budding young actor, Charlton Heston played in this town. The great preacher R. A. Torry died there. The highest mountain east of the Rockies is near there, and the Blue Ridge Parkway, one of the most visited places in the national park system, almost circles Asheville.

Your attitude about your situation can either cause stagnation or stimulation. Oliver Wendell Holmes once said, "Minds stretched by a new idea never go back to their original dimensions." The opportunities are endless for good, wholesome, stimulating food for the mind. Use your imagination and put together a custom-made mind-stimulation program for yourself.

WEED AND FEED SPIRITUALLY

Unfortunately, Peter Marshall was right when he said, "Although the average American woman has advantages that pioneer women never knew—material advantages, education, culture, advances made by science and medicine—although the modern woman knows a great deal more about diets, health, germs, drugs, medicines, and vitamins than her grandmother did, there is one subject about which she does not know as much—and that is God."

"Give us this day our daily bread" is part of the Lord's Prayer that most of us have known since childhood. It is a prayer for physical bread, but it is also a prayer for spiritual bread.

The Scriptures teach us that Jesus Christ is the Bread of Life. Each time I partake of communion, I am reminded by the cup and the loaf of my total dependence upon Christ. Just as we are dependent upon physical bread and drink to survive, we are also dependent upon Jesus Christ for our spiritual nourishment.

How vitally important it is to weed and feed ourselves spiritually. A dieter's proverb says, "You are what you eat." We are spiritually what we feed our souls.

MALNOURISHED CHRISTIANS

Many Christians have poor spiritual diets. Some are spiritually weak because they are on a baby-food diet.

Hebrews 5:12b–14 (TLB) reads, "You are like babies who can drink only milk, not old enough for solid food. And when a person is still living on milk it shows he isn't very far along in the Christian life, and doesn't know much about the difference between right and wrong [discernment]. He is still a baby-Christian. You will never be able to eat solid spiritual food and understand the deeper things of God's Word until you become better Christians." Baby Christians not only like baby food but they like to be spoon-fed. They go from Bible study to Bible study, from seminar to seminar, from church to church, never taking the time to read and study the Word of God for themselves.

Every year in Yellowstone National Park after the tourist season is over and the snow falls, dozens of bear die by the side of the road. These bear have become so dependent on the handouts from tourists that their natural instincts to search for their own food have been impaired. So, they wait for easy food and die.

Christians who live from handout to handout, who depend on the spiritual experience of others, who listen to sermons, tapes, and seminars but do not study the Bible for themselves are living on "spiritual welfare."

Some Christians suffer from spiritual hypoglycemia. They love spiritual sweets and carbohydrates. They like the spiritual trimmings and desserts. But when deeper truths are taught or they are faced with a tough spiritual challenge or their lifestyle is questioned, they refuse nourishment or avoid it altogether.

Other Christians are spiritual anorexics. They are just slowly starving. They exercise vehemently by running from one spiritual event to another, but they don't eat. They see themselves as spiritually healthy and refuse nourishment because they are unaware of their impoverished spiritual condition. Because of their lack of spiritual nourishment, they lower their immunity against the wiles of the devil.

I have a friend who became a Christian about two years ago. She sought out a Bible-teaching church, read good books, and showed interest in a Bible study. But soon her busy social life and her job filled up her time and she no longer received the necessary spiritual nourishment. She is a nice person who doesn't really see the necessity for spiritual food so she is slowly starving spiritually.

Still others become spiritually sick because they go on spiritual fad diets. A certain book, speaker, or theological teaching becomes their latest fad. I knew a family who had all become followers of a certain Christian teacher and author. They read, studied, and discussed this man's teachings for years, slowly becoming more and more ingrown. Because there was little balance in their spiritual menu, this man's influence began to distort their faith.

Still other Christians are spiritual gluttons who are stuffed spiritually, filled to overflowing with facts, ideas, information, and personal testimonies but don't know what to do with them. They are often so stuffed they suffer spiritual indigestion. Since they have not really absorbed or assimilated this spiritual knowledge, they are unable to appropriate it in their daily lives. They are like David in all of Saul's heavy armor (see 1 Sam. 17). They just stand there not knowing what to do.

Having a healthy spiritual life means we take in, assimilate, absorb, and then testify to others what we have learned. What we really need for our spiritual growth and health is a balanced spiritual diet. Not feast or famine, not fasts or fads, but consistent, balanced, scriptural teaching which can be absorbed, assimilated and adapted as a part of us.

F. B. Meyer suggested having a little spiritual food at a time. He said that it is often better to have "shorter portions for daily study, to give us time to get all the juice and marrow out of what we read." Sometimes just a few verses offer us ample nourishment for a daily meal of truth. We often need to meditate all day on just one verse or a portion of a verse in order to really understand its meaning. This can be welcome news to the young mother, the busy student, or the business executive. But note that this should apply to "daily" study and should not provide an excuse to abandon the time set aside for deeper Bible study.

Feeding the Soul a Balanced Diet

Develop consistent, personal Bible reading and Bible study habits. I distinguish between the two because I believe Bible reading should be a daily habit whereas Bible study could be less frequent.

General MacArthur once told an American Bible Society visitor, "Never a day goes by, be I ever so tired, but I read the Bible before I go to bed." As a child, I remember my mother's keeping her Bible open on a table or the ironing board so she could read even one verse and meditate upon it during the day. Some find that morning is a good time to read the Bible. Not being a morning person, I prefer night when the work is done, the kids are in bed, and all is quiet.

In-depth Bible study may be something you are able to do once a week. For this, you will need tools: a table or desk, preferably one where you can leave your Bible open and your books handy; a good modern translation of the Bible; and a good Bible study book such as *Halley's Bible Handbook* or *What the Bible Is All About*, by Henrietta Mears. Eventually you may wish to add to your library a Bible dictionary, a Bible almanac, and a set of commentaries. There are quite a few commentaries available, but *Through the Bible* by Vernon McGee is particularly helpful and practical.

Get Involved in a Bible-Teaching Church

I cannot stress enough the importance of a Bible-teaching church, especially if you have children. I have friends who stay in churches where they are starving spiritually because they don't want to "make waves" or because they have been there for "so long" or because their father was one of the founders. If you and your family are not being spiritually fed the deep and practical truths from the Word of God, you might as well stay home and sleep.

If you and your children were starving physically and you heard of a place that was giving away food, you would not hesitate to take your children there twice a day even if it were far away and not the most convenient for the family schedule. How much more important it is to find a church where you are fed spiritually at least once a week!

Choose Carefully Your Reading and Listening

In America today, so much spiritual material is available that often we can become confused about what is healthy and what should be avoided. There are seminars, conferences, and programs plus hundreds of hours of television and radio time given over to religious broadcasting. There are literally thousands of religious books and much religious literature to choose from.

Obtain Wisdom

The Scriptures warn us of "false teachers" who come in "sheep's clothing" (see Matt. 7:15–20). But it is not always easy to determine who is who or what is what. This is where the discerning power of the Holy Spirit comes in. In James 1:5, we read, "If any of you lacks wisdom, let him ask of God." We must rely on the wisdom of God revealed through His Word, the Holy Spirit, and trusted men and women of God to help us make the right decisions.

Through His Word. If you spend time in the Word of God, you will know when something is said that is not in agreement with Scripture. D. L. Moody once said, "If a person neglects the Bible there is not much for the Holy Spirit to work with."

My mother told me of a friend who once visited Scotland Yard and happened to meet the man whose job it was to inspect and identify counterfeit coins.

"You must spend hours studying and concentrating on these counterfeits," this friend observed.

"Oh no," replied the gentleman, "on the contrary, I spend hours concentrating on those that are real."

If we concentrate on the Word of God, we will recognize the counterfeits.

Through the Holy Spirit. Be sensitive to the promptings of the Spirit. A woman's intuition and discernment go hand in hand, providing valuable insights and perceptions. If you doubt something you hear or read, don't ignore it; trust your intuition, take it as a prompting of the Spirit, and check it out with the Word of God.

Often as I read certain "religious" or even "Christian" books or attend certain seminars, I suddenly have a feeling that something is amiss. Something is said or done that is not in accordance with scriptural principles, and my spiritual antennae go up. I may not be able to identify or articulate what is wrong right away, but since it is more a feeling or intuition, which is often discernment, I begin to pray and ask the Holy Spirit to show me what is wrong. Then I check it out with the Scriptures. If I can't find the answer myself, I go to a man or woman of God and ask for his or her help.

Through Trusted Men and Women of God. I look for spiritual guidance from men and women who have known the Lord Jesus many years and who rely on the Word of God as their authority. They advise me about which are the better speakers and Bible studies, and they give me the names of books and authors who have blessed them.

Many of our finest Bible teachers broadcast daily or at least weekly over TV and radio. Many also have available cassette tapes. But don't waste time being spoon-fed "baby food." Listen to solid Bible teaching taught by men and women of God (such as Chuck Swindoll, Stuart Briscoe, Warren Wiersbe, Elisabeth Elliott, Jill Briscoe, Charles Stanley) who believe the Bible is both the inspired Word of God and the road map for practical Christian living.

Look for a good Bible study to attend. There are national groups such as Bible Study Fellowship that offer excellent, in-depth Bible teaching. For information write: Bible Study Fellowship, 19001 Blanco Road, San Antonio, Texas, 78258.

Read choice Christian books. Much of what is written today is good, but again, we need to read the *classics*. I will give a list of books that have enriched my life at the end of this chapter.

However great these works and writers may be, they were never meant to take the place of Scripture. Don't ever allow even the greatest book to keep you from *the* Book itself.

> His thoughts said, "I have been reading a spiritual book and I am confused and tired of trying to understand." His Father said, "Leave that book and read the Book that thou lovest best; thou wilt find it much simpler."[1]

These other works are never to take the place of Scripture. They are only to help us better understand Scripture.

It is once again springtime in Florida. Yes, we do have a spring. You might not notice it if you came for a visit, but we who live here all year see the subtle changes. The new leaves begin to push the old ones off, and so we experience fall raking in spring. We look for the bottle brush tree dripping with the unusual red blooms which give it its name; the yellow trumpet tree; the red, pink, and white oleander; the multi-shaded hibiscus. The scent of jasmine is in the air, the birds are busily building their nests, and yes, its weed and feed time again.

Sometimes it seems overwhelming. There is never an end to what needs to be done in a garden, but little by little, day by day, we keep our gardens beautiful.

So it is with our souls' garden. The Lord will cultivate the soil, He will provide the tools, He will trim and prune when necessary, but He gives us the responsibility of fertilizing. Our job is to *weed and feed*!

Additional Reading

Confessions of St. Augustine, by Saint Augustine (New York: Macmillan, 1961).

The Everlasting Man, by G. K. Chesterton (Westport, CT: Greenwood, 1974). (Eerdman's has now published a collection of his better works.)

Foxe's Book of Martyrs, by George Foxe (Springsdale, PA: Whitaker House, 1981).

A *Serious Call to a Devout and Holy Life*, by William Law (Wilton, CT: Morehouse, 1968). This is not easy reading, but Tyndale has just published a shorter, edited, contemporary version called *A Serious Call to Holy Living*, by Marvin D. Hinten.

The Practice of the Presence of God, a small delightful book by Brother Lawrence (Grand Rapids: Baker Books, 1975).

Mere Christianity, by C. S. Lewis (Westwood, NJ: Barbour and Co., 1985). In fact, anything by C. S. Lewis, George MacDonald, Andrew Murrey, F. B. Meyer, R. A. Torry, and Charles Spurgeon offers excellent reading.

The Christian's Secret of a Happy Life, by Hannah W. Smith (Springsdale, PA: Whitaker House, 1983).

Biographies of great men and women of God, such as *Hudson Taylor's Spiritual Secret* (Chicago: Moody) or *Shadow of the Almighty* (New York: Harper and Row, 1979).

Books of prayer, such as *A Diary of Private Prayer*, by John Baillie (New York: Scribner, 1984).

Devotional books, such as *My Utmost for His Highest*, by Oswald Chambers (New York: Dodd, Mead, 1985), or *Streams in the Desert*, compiled by Mrs. Charles Cowman (Grand Rapids: Zondervan, 1983).

Some of these books may not be easy to find—in fact, some are out of print—but what fun it is to look for them in secondhand bookstores or book booths at antique shows.

Other Christian authors I enjoy are Lloyd J. Ogilvie, Catherine Marshall, J. I. Packer, Phillip Keller, Richard Foster, Eugene H. Peterson, Chuck Colson, and Eugenia Price.

9 *How Can I Be Beautiful?*

When I was a young girl, Daddy once came home and told us about this absolutely gorgeous woman he had met. Of course we were all curious about what she looked like, but the only adjective we could get out of him was "gorgeous." We imagined all sorts of things: long blond hair, a beautiful hourglass figure, big expressive eyes. Several years later, Mother had an opportunity to meet this "gorgeous" woman. She was not what we children had envisioned. She turned out to be rather plain, almost nondescript physically. But she was warm, enthusiastic, loving, caring of others. She had a good sense of humor, was positive, and opened her heart and home to others. This woman exuded a loveliness that *made* her gorgeous.

Christian Dior once said, "There is no such thing as an ugly woman, just those who do not know how to make themselves attractive." He was speaking of physical beauty, but this is also true of inner beauty. There are many Christian women who possess the possibility of inner beauty and loveliness and are just not attractive. They lack Christian appeal. They have negative, complaining spirits. They are dull and uninteresting. They lack humor, compassion, tact, and insight. They lack the "gentle, quiet spirit" that is pleasing to the Lord. This inner unattractiveness soon manifests itself outwardly and no amount of makeup or expensive clothing can make them beautiful.

When I was about ten years old, Daddy decided that Mother needed more help in the home and thought a Swiss governess was just the thing. On his next trip to Europe he interviewed two or three candidates. They all possessed about the same qualifications, so he chose one from the German part of Switzerland because of "the twinkle in her eye."

A few months later she arrived. It didn't take us children long to realize that the "twinkle" was actually a wicked gleam. She reminded us of the wicked witch of the west from *The Wizard of Oz*, and it soon became obvious she did not like children, especially American children. I do not remember ever seeing her smile and she never encouraged or praised us. She tried to force upon us a strict, unbending schedule which included little fun and less freedom, and she even forbade talking at the table, even when we ate in the kitchen. She had little respect for my mother and practically ignored her, only taking her orders from Daddy (his frequent absences made this rather inconvenient for my mother).

Although she was a Christian, she possessed no Christian attractiveness. She lacked a "gentle, quiet spirit" and was in more ways than one quite unattractive. Needless to say, she didn't last long in our home. However, because my parents had guaranteed her a job for three years they were responsible for finding her another place of employment. Because of her "unattractiveness," she was asked to leave several different places of employment over the next three years.

Most of today's role models are glamorous and thin. Even the nightly news is presented by handsome, athletic-looking men or young, apparently flawless women. And yet Dr. Isaac Rubin, the well known psychoanalyst, said in one journal column, "Genuine beauty has far less to do with external packaging than with inner life."

INTERIOR DESIGN

For a Christian woman, *interior design* is the key to genuine beauty.

Mother once took a poll. She asked several of her young bachelor friends which they would prefer to have in a wife: scenery or atmosphere. Without exception, they all replied "Scenery." She then polled her married male friends, asking them the same question. Without exception, they all replied, "Scenery would be nice, but atmosphere is essential."

True beauty is from the inside. When a woman is beautiful inside, she will have a certain glow, a comeliness, a charm about her. She will exude enthusiasm and confidence. She will possess a certain self-assurance and contentment. The outward beauty of a woman is only a mirror of the inward ageless loveliness of her heart and soul.

The Scripture says that a "woman that feareth [has reverential trust in] the Lord shall be praised" (Prov. 31:30 KJV). Fear of and total trust in the Lord is the first step toward obtaining inner beauty.

A Beautiful Woman Has a Gentle Quiet Spirit

First Peter tells us, "Don't be concerned about the outward beauty that depends on jewelry, or beautiful clothes, or hair arrangement. Be beautiful inside, in your hearts, with the lasting charm of a *gentle and quiet spirit* which is so precious to God" (1 Pet. 3:3–4 TLB, italics added).

I am not gentle and quiet by nature. Consequently, I have spent the better part of my life struggling to develop a "gentle, quiet spirit" since I was certain this fault of character was displeasing or at least disappointing to my Lord. I would often wonder why God had made me the way I am if He loves quietness and gentleness. It was not until recently that I began to discover that this "quiet, gentle spirit" is not so much nature or personality as it is an inward attitude of the heart. It is that quiet assurance that emanates from a heart that has placed its *total trust* and *complete confidence* in the Lord. This is the quiet gentle spirit that is pleasing to our heavenly Father even though our natures and personalities may not be naturally tranquil or placid.

A Beautiful Woman Is Serene

Inner beauty is the result of inner quietness.

An artist was once asked to paint an illustration of the word *peace*. He thought and thought. He thought of a gentle sunset, a still lake at dawn, a mountain meadow in springtime; but none seemed appropriate. Finally he painted a fierce storm. The clouds were dark and thick, the waves high and rough, the trees bent over by the strength of the wind. And in the corner, under a large overhanging rock, a small bird slept peacefully in its nest.

Serenity in the height of the storm is the inner serenity of a quiet, gentle spirit. It is being confident that God is leading us even though we are in utter darkness. It is holding fast in the midst of terrible suffering to the truth that "All things do work out for good to those that love God" (Rom. 8:28). It is clinging to "the Rock that is higher than I" (Ps. 61:2) when all around us is shifting.

I once had a small poodle named Cedrick who was like my shadow. He followed me everywhere. Whenever I left the house, he would beg to go with me. Once when we left for several months, we took Cedrick along. He didn't know where we were going or for how long; he had no indication that his bowl of food would be waiting for him or that he would find another comfy corner to call his own. He only knew that I was going and since he loved and trusted me, he jumped into the car and lay peacefully and contentedly on the floor at my feet. This simple faith and confidence pleased me. Thus is our heavenly Father pleased when we show simple faith by lying peacefully at His feet.

Scripture tells us to become more like children. Children have the ability to trust. Remember when you were small, and your daddy put you high up on the counter in the kitchen and said, "Jump"? At first you were a bit afraid, but because you loved and trusted him, you let go and jumped. Let go, and jump into your heavenly Father's everlasting arms.

One of my favorite Bible stories is the one where Jesus and his disciples were crossing Lake Galilee in a small fishing boat. (See Mark 4:35–41.) It was a quiet evening and soon Jesus fell asleep. Suddenly, a fierce storm arose, threatening their small craft. The wind tossed and the waves beat, filling the boat with water. The disciples were terrified. They rushed to the back of the boat where Jesus was asleep on a pillow and shook him. "Don't you care that we are going to perish?" they shouted over the noise of the storm. Jesus quietly got up and stilled the storm. Then he turned to his disciples and asked with obvious disappointment, "Why are you so fearful? Why do you have so little faith?"

The disciples had seen the power of God manifested daily as they walked with Jesus along the dusty roads of Palestine and yet they lost their serenity when the storm hit them because they failed to rely upon H*is presence*. Jesus was with them in the boat and Jesus is with us. Jesus always accompanies His children through the storms.

The disciples were also fearful because they failed to rely upon H*is promise*. At the beginning of the story, Jesus had said, "Let us go to the other side." He had already promised a safe arrival. The Scriptures are full of the promises of God. We, too, have been promised a safe arrival if not necessarily a smooth voyage.

The disciples also failed to rely upon H*is power*. Even though they had seen the power of God demonstrated again and again as Jesus healed the sick and caused the blind to see, they failed to rely upon it. We, too, have seen God's power in our lives, yet during difficult times we fail to rely upon it.

We experience serenity as we abide in His presence, trust in His promises, and rely upon His power. This inner loveliness of serenity will soon overflow and bear other visible fruit.

A *Beautiful Woman* Is *Confident*

Inner beauty is being confident of God's love for you and His working in your life, confident, as the apostle Paul put it, in the fact that "He which began the good work in your life will continue to bring it to completion" (Phil. 1:6). Women who are blessed with certainties, who know who they are and know that they are loved, have a certain poise and confidence about them that is beautiful.

When you fall in love and are certain that the one you love also loves you, then you are confident enough to give evidence of your love. When was the last time you went to a wedding and came away talking about the ugly bride? Someone once said that there is no cosmetic for beauty like happiness, and all women are beautiful when they are happy *in love*.

I once knew a young woman who was quite homely. She was neither tall nor short. She had mousy brown hair and nondescript eyes. Her skin lacked luster and was flawed by a few acne scars. However, she did possess an inner beauty, which was discovered by a young man in her church. They fell in love and announced their engagement a few months later. I saw her soon afterward, and I couldn't believe the difference. Her skin glowed and her eyes sparkled, she was lovely.

So it is with God's love. He says, "I have loved you with an everlasting love" (Jer. 31:3). A woman who knows she is loved is beautiful.

Once we are certain of God's love for us and His acceptance of us, it is easy to manifest our love for Him to others. When we are in love with the Lord Jesus, it will show. There will be softness instead of sternness, gentle, loving expressions instead of hard ones. Anxiety and worry lines will diminish. We will have confidence and experience contentment. There will be a smile on our face and peace in our hearts.

BEAUTY IS A VERB

I once read an article in TV *Guide* in which an American journalist living in France compared European women to American women. He said that most European women possessed a charm that American women lacked because European women gave the impression they were more interested in the person they were with than in themselves. American women, however, seemed to care more about the impression they were making. They were more conscious of themselves than they were of their company. Now, this may or may not be true, but it illustrates my point. When we are freed from ourselves, we can give our attention to the care and concern of others.

A beautiful woman is one who has a servant spirit. She allows the beauty of the Lord Jesus to flow from her unselfconsciously and is willing to be available to others. She allows the Holy Spirit to cultivate in her the fruits of the Spirit, love, joy, peace, patience, kindness, goodness, faithfulness, gentleness, and self-control (see Gal. 5:22). These fruits are evidence of the beauty of Christ within her and she manifests and expresses them through her actions and mode of being.

Beauty is an action verb.

A *Beautiful Woman Is Patient*

A woman with Christian beauty bears trials calmly and without complaining. She is slow to react when provoked. She is steadfast under difficult or adverse circumstances. Paul described such a woman in Second Corinthians: "In everything she does she tries to show that she is a true minister of God. She patiently endures suffering and hardship and trouble of every kind" (see 6:4 TLB).

When Stephan and I were living outside Paris, I invited some of our unbelieving friends to come for dinner to meet Mother, who was visiting at the time. During the day, Mother received a telephone call from home. She was faced with some very disturbing news concerning one of my brothers far away on the other side of the world. I immediately asked her if she wanted me to cancel dinner to which she graciously replied no. Instead, Mother gave her anxieties to the Lord.

My friends arrived, and we enjoyed dinner together. It was late before they left, but Mother's smile never faded and the peace in her heart could be felt. Some time later, my friends remarked, "The thing which impressed us the most about your mother was the peace she emitted." Mother's inner beauty shone forth even in the midst of difficulty.

Paul told us in Galatians "not [to] be weary in well doing: for in due season we shall reap, if we faint not" (Gal. 6:9 KJV). A few days ago, a friend of mine who is a new Christian, called to share with me her reward for patience. She and her husband were having difficulties with one of their children.

"Gigi," she exclaimed, "the other night we had a confrontation, and I handled it so well, I never lost my temper. I just expressed love while quietly remaining firm."

Then she went on to express her joy over the fact that her husband had noticed a change in the way she dealt with problems. "My husband even complimented me on my patience," she said with obvious pleasure.

God rewards such patience. He tells us in James that the reward of unwearied patience is the crown of life (James 1:12).

A *Beautiful Woman* Is *Loving*

Love is *doing*, it is showing tenderness and unselfish concern for others. Love *is* obedience.

"A new commandment I give unto you, That ye love one another; as I have loved you" (John 13:34 KJV). Love is *not* a feeling. It is a decision. Love continues to *do* regardless of feelings.

The dear wrinkled and worn face of Mother Teresa of Calcutta is beautiful. There is no doubt she is a loving woman, and yet she and her Sisters of Charity may not always *feel* love toward all of the dying men and women of India nor for the victims of AIDS in San Francisco and New York, but she says she is compelled out of obedience to her Lord to feed the poor and care for the sick. She has made the decision to love.

One day Jerushah, then three, and I were discussing love. Suddenly she said, "Mama, I know what love is. It is the same word as heart."

A beautiful woman has a big heart.

A *Beautiful Woman* Is *Joyful*

Webster defines joy as "a feeling of great pleasure or happiness that comes from success, good fortune, or a sense of well-being." But for Christians, joy is not necessarily synonymous with happiness. We are not promised success or good fortune or a good feeling in Scripture, but we are promised joy (see Ps. 126:5). Difficulties are inevitable but misery is a choice.

Joy is an attitude of the heart, a decision of the mind. We should be able to say as David did in the Psalm, "My soul *shall* be joyful in the Lord" (Ps. 35:9, italics added). He found his joy in the presence of God and exclaimed, "In thy presence is fullness of joy" (Ps. 16:11 KJV). My mother is a joyful woman. With Daddy gone so much of the time, she couldn't have been always "happy" yet she was always joyful. After her book of poetry, *Sitting by My Laughing Fire*, was published, someone asked me why her poetry tended to be introspective and even a bit sad at times, revealing many of the valleys of her life. I thought about this and then answered, "Because with us, Mother shared the sunshine, the rain she saved for her pen."

Mother could claim with Nehemiah that the joy of the Lord was her strength (Neh. 8:10). Someone expressed it so well when he said, "Joy is the flag flown from the castle of the heart when the king is in residence."

A *Beautiful Woman* Is *Kind*

The story has been told of Somerset Maugham's mother who was an extraordinarily beautiful woman married to an extraordinarily ugly man. When a family friend once asked how such a beautiful woman could have married such an ugly man she replied, "He has never once hurt my feelings."

Emerson said so well that "where we fail to be loving, we fail to be wise." A beautiful woman is quick to manifest simple deeds of kindness, thoughtfulness, and unselfishness. One of my favorite reminders of this is Amy Carmichael's poem:

I ask Thee for a selfless love
Through constant watching wise
And a heart at leisure from itself
To soothe and sympathize.

A Beautiful Woman Is Faithful

It costs to be faithful. It cost Abraham, it cost Esther, it cost Daniel, it cost Stephen, Peter, and Paul. Does it cost you anything to be faithful to your Lord? He does not expect greatness or perfection but only faithfulness.

During the Civil War, at Altoma Pass the fort which was being held by General Corse was besieged by the enemy under General Hood who demanded that the northerners surrender. General Corse refused. Many casualties were suffered, and the situation seemed hopeless. Still the defenders remained faithful. Then a white signal flag across the valley waved this message, "Hold the fort, for I am coming." General Sherman was on his way to relieve the beleaguered and faithful soldiers. So it is with us. The Lord is on His way, and one day He will say "Well done, good and faithful servant" (Matt. 25:21).

A Beautiful Woman Is Self-controlled

A beautiful woman is not controlled by her circumstances or her compulsions, nor by her impulses or emotions, but she is controlled by the Holy Spirit.

Author Elisabeth Elliot is such woman. Elisabeth has had a difficult life by anyone's standards. Married to Jim Elliot, who was murdered by the Auca Indians, she became a widow for the first time while still very young. Instead of allowing sorrow and hate to control her life, she submitted to the Holy Spirit and returned with her infant daughter to the jungles as a missionary to the same people who had killed her husband. She raised her daughter by herself and later married a much older man. They were not married too long before they discovered he was ill, so she spent months caring for him until his death. Through these and many other difficult experiences, Elisabeth has discovered the truth that "discipline is a glad surrender" (the title of a book that Elisabeth Elliot has written on the subject of discipline). She says, "Discipline is a wholehearted yes to the call of God."

Elisabeth is now married again and a grandmother. Not long ago I was eating lunch with her and several other women. As she spoke with the woman next to her, I realized that Elisabeth is truly a woman who has not allowed the circumstances of her life to control her. Through discipline she has submitted to God's will, allowing Him to bring all her emotions and impulses under His control. Thus she radiates both inward and outward beauty. Elisabeth is a beautiful woman.

If we are to take seriously the call to discipleship, we have to take seriously the call to discipline. Paul told us in Corinthians, "Every man [woman] that striveth for the mastery is temperate in all things" (1 Cor. 9:25 KJV).

None of the characteristics of a beautiful woman comes naturally or instantaneously. They are the fruit that is produced in our lives through the influence of the indwelling Holy Spirit of God. A beautiful woman also has a humble, teachable spirit and can only obtain her beauty through an intimate relationship with Jesus Christ—a relationship over which He is Lord. He is the vinedresser who plants, prunes, fertilizes, and cultivates this fruit. He must be in charge of the vineyard or the fruit will not flourish.

If these adjectives don't yet describe you, don't be discouraged. Fruit has to be grown and this takes time and practice. The story is told of a young Christian from a remote Korean village who learned the whole Sermon on the Mount by heart and then tramped many miles to recite it to a missionary. When the young man had finished, the missionary encouraged him to put it into practice.

"But that is the way I learned it," the young man replied. "At first I tried to remember it, but it wouldn't stick. So then I tried this: I learned a verse, and then I went out and practiced it on a neighbor. That way, I found it would stick."

OBTAINING INNER BEAUTY

We would all agree that we would like to see the attributes of inner beauty manifested in our daily lives. But how do we become beautiful women? I have found these steps to be essential.

Make Sure of Your Personal Relationship with the Lord

You cannot spill out what you do not have within. Have you placed your confidence in the Lord and Him alone? Do you trust Him totally? Are you resting in His love?

I have a friend Ann, who is a lovely, deeply commited Christian. She has a wonderful Christian husband and three bright, handsome, caring sons. But it was not always so. A few short years ago, her marriage was almost beyond repair and she was in a mental hospital contemplating suicide.

Ann met her husband while in school; they fell in love and were married rather quickly. Her husband soon joined his family's luxury yacht-building business. Ann seemed to have it all. She was young and physically attractive. She had a husband who loved her and a charming, healthy child. She had a beautiful, expensive home and money in the bank. But something was lacking.

She was forced into social circles that were unfamiliar to her since she came from a simple family. Because of her background she felt inadequate and suffered from low self-esteem. The more inadequate she felt, the more she leaned on her husband, a very busy man with long hours. Her demands on his attention were stifling and soon the pressures and tensions began to take their toll.

Although my friend was kind and giving, she was possessive of those she loved. She placed all her hopes and reasons for living in the people around her, and one by one they began to disappoint her and even desert her. Her husband moved out, she began to lose touch with reality, and finally she ended up in the hospital.

One day a friend introduced her to Jesus Christ. As the weeks went by, she began to ask questions, and it wasn't long before she realized she needed to place her trust in the Lord Jesus who never disappoints anyone. She quietly opened her heart's door and asked the Lord Jesus to come into her life.

Nothing dramatic happened at first. But as the months passed she became involved in a prayer group, then a Bible study. She joined a church and became active in it. She began reading the Word of God and spent time in prayer. Slowly as she walked hand-in-hand with the Lord, her character began to change. Where she had been a nag to her husband, begging him to stay at home more, she became his sweetheart; thus, he wanted to be home more. Where she had often been negative and cross with the children, she became positive and encouraging. Her husband saw these changes and also gave his heart to the Lord Jesus. Together, they put the Lord first in their lives and their marriage was healed. Where the home had been full of unpleasantness and tension, it was filled with love and warmth.

An active woman, my friend learned to pace herself and give herself time to grow. She no longer thought of herself and her inadequacies and failures. Instead she began to focus her attention on others and how she could help meet their needs. If a friend needed counseling, she made an appointment with a counselor and paid the bill; if a friend needed encouragement, she sent a beautiful bouquet of flowers; if a friend needed the Lord, she took him to church and then to lunch.

Several years have now passed, and many come to her for advice and counsel. Because of her husband's business, she has a real ministry helping those who have "everything to live with and nothing to live for." Those meeting her for the first time invariably describe her as "beautiful." Her beauty is the result of her placing her trust in the Lord Jesus Christ.

Allow God to Be the Gardener of Your Life

You must allow the Holy Spirit to redesign and rearrange you so that you can bear much fruit. This may not be pleasant. He may have to prune and trim a bit. Gardening manuals tell us that pruning is often necessary for the health of the vine since it often restores a vine or increases its strength and production. Pruning is also necessary to enhance the beauty of a vine.

I have a lovely little hibiscus tree that had so many blooms it looked like a bouquet of yellow flowers outside my kitchen window. I knew sometime ago that it should have been pruned, but I kept putting it off since I would have to cut some of the flowers and destroy its beauty. I failed to realize that pruning is often necessary for future loveliness and that it even enhances beauty. I let the little tree go unpruned until it has become all misshapen.

There have been many times in my life when the Holy Spirit found it necessary to prune me. Remember the night that I found my home flooded? The Lord pruned me way back through that experience. He removed my lovely home and temporarily my beautiful things were gone. He even allowed Stephan to be away in the Swiss army for six weeks. He permitted me to live in a bare, cold, inconvenient place where because of my circumstances I felt imprisoned. I had no friends, no family, only the three small children for company. Soon even my health was pruned and I found it very difficult to care for the children because of illness.

At that time the experience seemed overwhelming and almost unbearable, but the Lord used it to strengthen my inner character. Sitting in that big, red wingback chair, I spent my days and much of my nights reading my Bible and talking with Him. In looking back I can see the value of that experience. I discovered that I could be alone yet not be lonely because when Jesus is all you have, you soon discover that He is all you need.

This small experience strengthened my faith. If He was there then, He would also be there when I faced even more difficult times. And I could rest assured that if I grew through this experience I would continue to grow through the difficult experiences ahead. Because of this, I have learned to look at difficulties as challenges.

Don't Dodge Difficulties

I once joined an exercise club. I paid my fee, signed my contract, filled out my goal card, and bought the necessary clothing. The first day went well. The equipment wasn't heavy and I breezed through. *Nothing to it*! I thought. I kept up the same easy pace all week.

The next week, my weight load on the machines was increased. I moaned and groaned but still persisted. The third week the load got heavier. I groaned louder and perspired more. I went home exhausted. I began to find excuses to avoid the club. I began to dodge the difficulty. Soon I quit altogether. Of course, my goals were aborted also: my tummy is still not flat and my thighs are still flabby.

Often the difficulties in our lives are the very thing God uses to stretch and strengthen our spiritual muscles and to develop inner beauty and depth of character. Mother once remarked to me that many of the women she knew who were married to difficult men had such beautiful characters. Could it be that they had allowed the Holy Spirit to develop their inner character and beauty through difficulty?

One such friend was married to a busy executive. When he arrived home in the evening, she would literally jump up and run to greet him, throwing her arms around his neck in a warm, loving welcome. But this husband was difficult to live with. For example, he would then read his mail, absently discarding the letters that held little interest on the floor. His wife would patiently pick them up and put them back in order. Once when my mother was at their home for dinner, he took one look at the soup she served and remarked, "Why don't you keep your dirty dish water in the kitchen?" But mother's friend continued to show love and demonstrate kindness.

My friend Darlene is married to an interesting, articulate, and lovable man. Although he doesn't mean it, he has the bad habit of snapping at his wife. He even sometimes embarrasses her by speaking harshly to her in front of others. But instead of getting offended or snapping back, she always responds sweetly, choosing either to ignore his rudeness or to laugh good-naturedly and thus break the tension. Everyone is aware of her sweetness and her gentle, loving spirit. She is an inspiration to all who know her and many seek her counsel.

We often question the difficulties in our lives and yet, as someone once said, "Difficulties are a wonderful fertilizer to the roots of character."

The first chapter in the book of James addresses this subject. James said, "Is your life full of difficulties . . . then be happy, for when the way is rough, your patience has a chance to grow. So let it grow, and don't try to squirm out of your problems for, when your patience is finally in full bloom, then you will be ready for anything, strong in character, full and complete" (James 1:2–4 TLB). Charles Spurgeon noted that "Many owe the grandeur of their lives to their tremendous difficulties."

Inner beauty is the beauty and loveliness of God within us, and a woman who possesses this beauty will not necessarily be aware of her loveliness. But those around her will see the beauty and sense the atmosphere.

When we are clothed in the righteousness of God and are abiding in Him and living a life of obedience to Him, then His beauty will be our clothing and those around us will say, "The king's daughter is all glorious within." Inner beauty is His interior design.

10 Would You Like a Vacation?

The sand was warm and soothing against my skin. I listened to the waves gently lapping the shore. A small sailboat, its white sails a sharp contrast against the vivid blue of the sea and sky, made its way slowly to the steep volcanic island just off shore. A graceful cruise ship was slipping lazily over the horizon and a few billowy clouds played hide and seek with the sun. What a racket the tiny yellow "sugar" birds were making this morning as they darted in and out of the surrounding trees, busily attacking the generous amount of orange marmalade I had left on the terrace after finishing my breakfast of croissant and coffee.

I closed my eyes. The soft tropical breeze caressed my warm body and I felt wonderful. I was away from the children, away from the noise and pressures of life, away from all of my responsibilities. No dishes to wash, no dirty clothes, no diapers, no deadlines—just sun, surf, and serenity. I couldn't help feeling a little envious of those privileged few who possess the resources to experience this solitude, this seclusion from society, whenever they have the desire and not just on very special occasions.

My life has become so hectic, so busy, that too often I experience the "barrenness of busyness." My muddled mind and stretched nerves feel a great need for rest and relaxation and my starved spirit screams for solitude and spiritual refreshment. I get so caught up in the mundane things of everyday life, that my soul and spirit suffer. Many a day rushes past and I fall into bed at night and say, "Well, Lord, here I am again. I haven't had much time to be with you today. You say that we are to be still and know that you are God, but this is the first time today that I have been able to be still. But I do love you." About that time, exhausted, I fall asleep.

Since lying lazily on a beautiful tropical beach is a rather rare experience for most of us, I decided to see if it was possible to discover other ways of experiencing some of the same benefits I enjoyed on this lovely vacation. As I examined my situation more closely, I realized I really didn't need a bonafide vacation as often as I thought I did. Yes, it would be nice just to "get away" whenever I felt overwhelmed. But it would also be an escape from reality, and I needed to face the facts and work within my circumstances.

One night at the supper table, my daughter, then four years old, who sits beside me, was saying something under her breath. I bent down to hear what she was saying, and above the noise of the others, I heard her whisper, "Peace and quiet, peace and quiet, peace and quiet."

"Who has peace and quiet, darling?" I asked.

"No one has peace and quiet," she replied.

She was right. With ten people in our household, there is little peace and less quiet.

What I really needed was to find a way to experience rest and refreshment in the midst of a hectic household. I decided to examine more closely if this was possible.

What?

Although each of us has a different set of circumstances, most of us live in a world where we are faced daily with an overload. Crowded cities and highways to contend with, tight schedules to keep, deadlines to meet, households to manage, budgets to balance, decisions to make, noise and nerves to cope with. We are also part of a society that equates busyness with productivity and thus success, so we feel guilty if we are not busy; and yet, we all have the need to experience balance in the midst of all our distractions.

When?

When was the last time you sat outside and simply enjoyed the night sounds—the crickets, the tree toads, the katydids? When was the last time you took a walk (not necessarily for exercise) and observed the small, intricate, almost hidden beauties of nature that few ever notice? The tiny exquisite wildflowers hidden beneath the fallen leaves or peeking out from behind a stone, the moss clinging to rocks, the rough brown or gray bark on the trees? When was the last time you bit into a ripe juicy peach or plump strawberry and took a moment to savour and enjoy its sweetness? When was the last time you looked up into the dark winter sky and felt the wet, soft snowflakes as they fell gently on your face? Or held your child, for no special reason, except to feel the softness of him or touch the damp curls and look into his bright eager eyes? When was the last time you lay in your husband's arms and thanked God for him, for his strength and warmth, protection and support?

From Creation, God instilled in us the need for rest and He set for us an example by resting Himself on the seventh day. We don't know why He created within us this need for rest and refreshment, but perhaps He wanted us to stop in the middle of our busy, hectic lives and be still and quiet long enough to know that He is God, that He is there, and that He dearly loves us. Perhaps because "He has given us richly all things to enjoy," He wants us to slow down long enough to appreciate and enjoy these manifestations of His love, all the marvelous things both large and small that He so lavishly gives to us for the express purpose of pleasure.

We all need these small quiet moments, but we often ignore this need until it is too late. Anxiety, depression, worry, stress, and many of our physical ailments are often symptoms of a body, soul, and spirit that has not obeyed this natural need for rest. Rest and refreshment is not a luxury, it is a necessity.

How?

I found myself ignoring this need in my life. I could tell by the way little things bugged me, or by the tone of my voice, or the way I responded to a child's plea for attention. I could tell by the way I overreacted to certain situations or the way I felt tired as soon as I awoke.

I was displeased with this situation. I knew that what I really desired was peace and that if I had it my life would manifest it in visible ways. I longed to get off the merry-go-round of busyness. But how could I manage this in the throes of my hectic life without abandoning my responsibilities. Once again I found myself on a beach, with the Lord, a few books, and some extra time to seek the answer to this question.

ATTITUDE OF HEART AND MIND

First of all I discovered that weariness of mind and spirit does not necessarily have to do with physical exhaustion. I can be rested physically and still suffer from mental and spiritual weariness.

My mother once told me of going away on a lovely vacation. She slept late, ate well, swam every day, and yet arrived home weary. She discovered that she had taken the time to refresh herself physically but not spiritually. Rest and refreshment is often part of an inward state of heart and mind.

William James, the great American psychologist, said, "The greatest discovery of my generation is that people can alter their lives by altering their attitudes of mind." The Scriptures say it this way: "Thou wilt keep him in perfect peace, whose *mind* is stayed on thee" (Isa. 26:3 KJV, italics added).

Take Advantage of Small Snatches of Time

I have an older friend who has lived a full, extremely active life and still keeps a schedule that would keep many a younger man exhausted. One of the secrets of this energy is that he can sleep anywhere, anytime, for just a few seconds and awake feeling totally refreshed.

I find this to be applicable emotionally and spiritually. By taking advantage of small snatches of mental, emotional, and spiritual refreshment, I can experience refreshment in the middle of chaos. I can be in the kitchen fixing dinner and experience joy over the fact that I have food to feed my children, a table to set, and a dishwasher to help with the cleanup. These few thoughts offer me brief moments of refreshment and reprieve from the work. After a hectic day I go to tuck the smaller children in for the night and offer thanks for the soft beds, the clean sheets, the safe environment. I may be totally physically exhausted, but my heart and mind are uplifted as I offer thanksgiving. I have found that *there is rest to be found in a positive attitude; there is rest to be found in a thankful heart.*

Take advantage of brief moments of time to refresh your body and spirit. For example, the other day, I was busy folding laundry and my two-year-old son came running into the house saying, "Mama, come here." Now I didn't want to go, nor did I wish to put off my work especially when I realized that "here" was the other side of the yard, but he was very insistent. I took his little hand and let him lead me to the lake where he had discovered a duck swimming.

On the way I noticed his blond curls blowing in the wind and his eager little face. He pointed to a jet vapor trail and asked me if it was a rocket (how does a two year old know about rockets?). I spent five minutes feeding the duck and enjoying my child, and when I returned to the laundry I was refreshed. Those few brief moments with my little son, which I might never recapture, had given me unexpected joy. I was uplifted and had renewed my motivation to continue folding clothes even though they were the same ones I had folded just two days before.

You may have a few minutes while your cake is baking to take a walk in your backyard. Breathe deeply, look up at the sky, listen to the wind in the treetops, and thank the Lord for at least two things. Or sit in your favorite overstuffed chair, turn on some music, and close your eyes for five minutes. Watch your children's favorite TV show with them and wash the dishes later in the evening. Our family enjoys the wild animal programs. We laugh at the monkeys, we shriek when the twenty-foot snake eats the rabbit, we hide our eyes when the lion attacks the antelope and we squeal with delight when the peacock opens his tail.

Find Joy in Happy Memories

We often spend the summer in North Carolina near my parents' home since we have the use of the small house in which I was raised. It is such fun to watch my children playing in the same stream, climbing the same trees, and walking the same trails I enjoyed as a child. After everyone is in bed, I will often go back into the living room and sit curled up on the sofa watching the embers die in the large stone fireplace until there is only a faint glow left. A flood of happy memories surrounds me and offers encouragement and refreshment to my spirit. I think of the Scripture verse which reads: "God who began the good work within me, [when as a child I gave my heart to Jesus in this very house] will keep right on helping me grow in his grace until his task within me is finally finished" (see Phil. 1:6 TLB). God won't give up on me.

In Scripture we are encouraged to take the time to reflect on happy memories for they give us joy and fill our hearts with thankfulness (see Phil. 1:3). For most of us, it will be these small snatches of refreshment, not prolonged vacations, that will save our sanity and spell survival. We need to learn to cultivate the habit of minute vacations. These small moments of time will mean the difference between drudgery and pleasure, discouragement and success.

But, we shouldn't stop there. Survival may depend on small snatches, but we should not be content with mere survival.

Plan for Rest and Relief

We need to plan for rest and relaxation. Many people I know never take vacations. "We can't afford it," they say, or "We don't have the time." I understand that they can't afford vacations on the soft sandy beaches or on the white snowy slopes. But I don't understand that they never take planned "time off."

I have friends who have been married for many years and have never taken a vacation together. Many vacations are expensive and do take time. But a weekend spent at a motel close by, or a day off together in the "big city," or a night alone at home with the children farmed out to friends can also be a vacation. Stephan and I have found that two or three shorter periods of time together are more beneficial than one longer time off. A weekend off or even an afternoon spent together breaks the routine, provides the needed relaxation, and gives us time alone to plan, discuss, and love at different intervals. Short trips are also easier to plan and arrange.

Single women also need "time off," planned alone or with friends away from roommates and office associates. A vacation is any planned time off for rest, refreshment, and a reprieve from work and responsibility.

Try loafing sometimes and don't feel guilty about it. This is especially hard for me. I can't even sit outside in the sun and read while the children swim, without soon discovering some weeds that need pulling, so I get up and start pulling. Yet there is a time for idleness. It is only wrong when it becomes a lifestyle.

Exercise

I personally am not athletic. I am like the man who said, "When I feel like exercising, I just lie down until it goes away." For me, exercising is sitting and reading. Yet I know that physical activity builds up one's strength and endurance and greatly relieves stress and tension, as well as improves one's figure.

Years ago when Stephan and I lived in France and I was under quite a bit of stress, my daddy suggested I try running to relieve my tension headaches. I drove the car around the circular drive of the large old French house we were renting until I discovered how many laps constituted a mile. Each evening I would run, which made a real difference in my headaches. I am ashamed to admit that during the winter I find myself too busy or too tired for regular exercise, but when summer comes, and I am on vacation with the children either in the mountains of North Carolina or at the beach, I take long walks daily and I have to admit that I feel better both emotionally and physically.

Dr. Garth Wood, a British psychoanalyst, says that just as the mind needs mental labor to remain alert, the body needs physical labor to remain healthy. He draws on recent evidence, which shows the psychological as well as physical benefits of regular exercise in combatting depression and enhancing self-respect.

If you're like me and don't care for organized physical fitness programs, you may enjoy working in your yard. I find pruning, clipping, and raking to be both physically rewarding and mentally relaxing. The important thing is to recognize the importance of some sort of exercise and make it a habit.

Stephan and I have a friend who is a businessman with heavy responsibilities. He felt a need for mental rest, refreshment, and physical exercise but had little time, so he had a Ping-Pong table installed in every boardroom of each of his offices around the world. Between appointments he takes a few minutes to play a vigorous game. Sometimes, if an appointment goes too long, one of his colleagues will call and remind him of an "appointment" in the boardroom. His client will quickly excuse himself, and our friend chuckles as he proceeds to the Ping-Pong table.

HOBBIES ARE HEALTHY

Some people feel that hobbies are a waste of time. I disagree. Nothing that gives your tired body, mind, or spirit needed rest is a waste of time.

My grandmother loved doing crossword puzzles, which she always kept handy, even in the glove compartment of her car. They also kept her from becoming frustrated if my grandfather, a busy doctor, was kept late. Some people keep a large jigsaw puzzle on a table. Others enjoy crafts, art, or gardening. When my mother is tired or under stress, she heads for the kitchen and produces a gourmet meal. My hobby is reading. Whatever your hobby, it should bring physical and mental relaxation and emotional enjoyment.

PRACTICAL METHODS TO ENCOURAGE REST

Both rest and relaxation require a conscious effort. If we are to experience rest, we also have to be practical. For example, I have learned not to run when I am outside and hear the telephone ringing. If I am in the yard, and the telephone rings, I make an effort to answer it, but I have decided not to drop everything and break my neck. I have discovered that if I miss it and the call was really important, the caller will call back. If it was not important, why leave what I was doing?

Mealtime should be a time of refreshment not only physically but also emotionally. Tension and disturbances should be kept to a minimum, so our family tries not to discuss stressful subjects or deal with discipline during meals.

Tension can also be caused by "information overload." The television screen brings into our living room a considerable amount of information, much of which is negative. This can cause frustration and even depression since usually there is little we can do about it. I have learned to limit the amount of information I allow myself to be subjected to and yet still retain a basic knowledge of what is going on.

Small practical ways to make your day more relaxing can quickly add up to hours of restful relief.

SAVOR THE SENSES

We no longer take the time to savor the five senses God gave us. When was the last time you took a moment to enjoy the softness of your sweater against your skin? Or the clean crisp sheets on your bed? When was the last time you sniffed the air and relished the smell of autumn leaves burning? Or baked a loaf of bread just for the pleasure of the odor emitting from your oven? Or sensed the warmth of your fireplace hearth as you cradled a cup of tea in your cold hands? We are usually in such a hurry that we no longer notice these small comforts and delights of life.

We rarely even enjoy eating. We rush to a fast food restaurant and hurriedly force some sort of junk food into our bodies or we stand in the kitchen while we are fixing dinner and munch on a quick sandwich that we have thrown together. I just stuffed down a couple of pieces of toast and a hardboiled egg while standing at the stove so I could get back to writing. How much more pleasant and restful it would be to fix a pretty salad or a bowl of homemade soup and sit down and appreciate each mouthful. I have begun to do this more often, sitting on my terrace, listening to the birds, and feeling the balmy breezes as I enjoy my lunch.

Not long ago Stephan and I experienced a rare half hour at home with no children. We were sitting on the sofa when suddenly we began to chuckle. We were hearing sounds we had never noticed before—the steady ticking of the grandfather clock, the soft humming of the refrigerator. Taking time to be conscious of and appreciate these senses causes us to become more conscious of God's love and constant care for us. This in turn gives rest to our spirit and refreshment to our souls. And we offer humble thanksgiving.

EXPRESS YOUR EMOTIONS

Tears often provide the much-needed outlet for pent-up frustration and sadness. Someone once said that "Tears are the window to heaven." Scripture tells us that "Laughter doeth good like a medicine." Notice how refreshed and relaxed you feel after a good hearty laugh? The other night Stephan and I went to a movie with good friends. Suddenly I whispered something to my friend, and we got the giggles. We laughed and laughed. It felt wonderful. Dwight Eisenhower once said, "The day that goes by without having some fun—the day you don't enjoy life—is not only unnecessary but unChristian."

Others express emotion through music, art, or writing. My mother expresses many of her emotions in her poetry. Many find it helpful to keep a diary. When I am upset I often share my feelings with my pen. Just being able to express my concerns helps to vent my feelings and clear the air.

GET THE PROPER REST

Sleep is vital. Nights when I have not slept for one reason or another make for difficult next days. After the birth of one of my children, I began to suffer from excruciating headaches. Nothing would relieve them and I found it more and more difficult to function. Finally the doctor discovered they were due to lack of sleep. As soon as this was corrected, my headaches disappeared.

As someone once said, "The best bridge between despair and hope is a good night's sleep." Each one of us requires a different amount of sleep, depending on his particular circumstances and responsibilities and his individual physical and emotional makeup. When you find yourself more tense, more nervous and anxious, or more cross and discouraged than normal, check your sleep habits.

Remember what one doctor recently said, "Good sleep is not the result of something you do immediately before retiring, but of a style of life and a manner of daily living. Our sleep reflects our total selves." Our lifestyles will have a great influence on how we sleep. The Scripture says it this way, "It is in vain that you rise up early and go late to rest, eating the bread of anxious toil; for he gives to his beloved sleep" (Ps. 127:2 RSV). When we really trust in our heavenly Father, our lifestyles reflect this. We can be assured that we "will both lie down in peace and sleep; for thou, Lord, only makest me dwell in safety" (Ps. 4:8).

PRACTICE THE PRESENCE OF GOD

Brother Lawrence, the seventeenth-century monk, developed a deep and rich spiritual life by "practicing the presence of God." This simply meant he was conscious of the fact that God was with him each and every moment. His simple philosophy, set forth in a little book called *The Practice of the Presence of God*, has given me great encouragement because Brother Lawrence's responsibilities were not in the pulpit but in the kitchen. He wrote: "Lord of all pots and pans and things . . . make me a saint by getting meals and washing up the plates." He also said, "The time of business does not with me differ from the time of prayer; and in the noise and clatter of my kitchen, while several persons are at the same time calling for different things, I possess God in as great tranquillity as if I were upon my knees at the blessed sacrament."

JESUS BREAKS

I like to call my small snatches of spiritual refreshment "Jesus breaks." When I can't do a Bible study or spend an hour in prayer, I can slip off alone for five minutes and spend them with Jesus. I have found this to be especially helpful when things are going from bad to worse and my nerves are stretched to the limit. I just talk to the Lord or meditate on one of the comforting, strengthening verses found in Scripture, such as, "Fear not; for I have redeemed thee, I have called thee by thy name; thou art mine" (Isa. 43:1 KJV).

I find it helpful to sit with my hands open in my lap in a receptive attitude of expectation. I simply receive His love, feel His presence, accept His strength, claim His promises, and then go back to whatever I was doing with renewed courage.

SABBATH REST

When I was a child, we kept a very strict Sabbath (Sunday). We were awakened by hymns playing over the intercom, and after a breakfast of coffee, orange juice, and sweetrolls, we dressed in our Sunday best and went to church. After church, lunch was served at home, often including someone who had no family, and then we would change our clothes and go out to play. However, we were not allowed to have friends over, and we could not play "secular" games or read "secular" books. Mother would sometimes read exciting stories of martyrs or missionaries and would teach us a few Bible verses.

We might take a walk together in the woods, or sit outside in the sun talking. We were allowed to have candy, chewing gum, and Cokes on Sunday, which were denied to us the rest of the week. Around five o'clock, my maternal grandparents would arrive for a pick-up supper and then we would gather around the baby grand piano and sing hymns. Then each child would snuggle close to an adult, and the Bible games would begin. Yes, Sundays were special.

I look back on these Sabbaths as days of joy, rest, and refreshment. Our Sundays were different from the rest of the week. We did as little work as possible, we rested from both work and play, we spent time with the Lord, and time together as a family.

Stephan and I are not quite so strict with our own little family. But we do still emphasize that Sunday is different from the rest of the week by encouraging worship, rest, and being together as a family.

The Sabbath rest was instituted at the time of Creation when after six days of work God rested. I don't believe for a moment that it was because He was tired. Nor do I think He ran out of things to create or ideas to execute. God was setting an example for all time. In fact, the Old Testament specifically set forth Sabbath laws.

The Sabbath is a time to stop our own thoughts and doings, and *reflect* upon the things of the Lord. God said, "If you call the Sabbath a delight and the LORD's holy day honorable, and if you honor it by not going your own way and not doing as you please or speaking idle words, then you will find your joy in the LORD" (Isa. 58:13b NIV). As we reflect upon the past week and its accomplishments we can measure and reevaluate them from eternity's perspective. God did this after He had created the world.

Gordon MacDonald quotes an Israeli rabbi who wrote about the Sabbath in a tourist brochure:

> Make the Sabbath an eternal monument of the knowledge and sanctification of God, both in the center of your busy public life and in the peaceful retreat of your domestic hearth. For six days cultivate the earth and rule it . . . but the seventh is the Sabbath of the Lord thy God . . . . Let [a man or woman] therefore realize that the Creator of old is the living God of today, that He watches every man and every human effort, to see how man uses or abuses the world loaned to him . . . . He is the sole architect to Whom every man and woman has to render an account of his week's labors.

Sabbath rest is essential for reflection, reevaluation, and real soul and body refreshment.[1]

DEEPER REST

"My soul is weary," Job cried. I am sure that from time to time we can all echo his words. However, the Lord Jesus Himself provided the antidote when He said, "Come unto me . . . and ye shall find rest unto your souls" (Matt. 11:28–30 KJV).

The other night the children and I were watching a program on television called "An African Waterhole." This program showed all the activities around a water hole in the African bush in midsummer when water is scarce. The need for water was so great the animals literally risked their lives twice a day when they approached the waterhole to satisfy their thirst in the presence of their predators. Our souls thirst for God, "for the living God" (Ps. 42:2), yet how much are we ready to give up or risk in order to drink of the living water? Are we willing to discipline our time? Are we willing to give up a few hours of television? Willing to set aside distractions? Willing to risk being misunderstood or ridiculed?

Not long ago, I found my soul parched. I felt dried up and spiritually shriveled. I decided to study certain spiritual disciplines, some of

God's resources that are available to us such as, prayer, Bible reading, meditation and solitude. I found that many blessings accompany these simple spiritual disciplines.

Prayer. Prayer has been a part of my life as far back as I can remember. Prayer was a way of life in our home. But not until I was twelve years old and went off to boarding school did prayer become a personal source of power. I learned to depend on God. I was alone. I no longer could run to Mother and Daddy with my problems. So I prayed about anything and everything. Nothing was too small for God to care about, and nothing was too large for Him to handle. I talked to Him as to my best friend. This practice has continued through the years and I will be forever grateful that I was taught to pray early in life.

Prayer is an exercise in communication. It must be practiced regularly, daily, just as communication with those we love must be practiced daily if the relationship is to grow. This can be done in many ways. Some find setting aside a special block of time is best, others use the time they spend driving to and from work, others prefer a few silent moments of prayer several times a day. I have found, that for my hectic lifestyle, I need to pray as the apostle Paul suggested, "without ceasing" my work. I pray as I wash dishes, scrub a child, run errands. I pray as soon as I awake and as I drift off to sleep. My communion with God is somewhat less formal than I would like it to be, and it is not always as consistent as it should be, but it is a persistent, continuing process.

Prayer is not a string of beautiful phrases, it is not a particular portion of time, it is not a position or posture—it is a way of life. It is as vital to our souls as breathing is to our bodies.

The important thing about prayer is to pray.

Bible reading. Along with prayer, I was taught early the joy of reading God's Word. Much of the unrest we experience is due to a lack of understanding or wisdom. We are often worried or anxious and we don't know what to do. Perhaps we lack purpose or direction. Perhaps we are experiencing hurt or loss, or maybe we're suffering from physical or emotional pain. Sometimes we lack strength and don't see how we are going to go on.

Within the pages of the Word of God we discover direction, comfort, cleansing, encouragement, wisdom, strength, and peace that passeth understanding. Psalm 119:11 says, "Thy word have I hid in mine heart, that I might not sin against thee." Verse 24 reads, "Thy testimonies are also my delight and my counselors." Verse 50 says, "This is my comfort in my affliction; for thy word hath quickened me." And verse 105 tells us that "Thy word is a lamp unto my feet and a light unto my path" (KJV).

The Word of God is His love letter to us, His instruction book, His road map, His shield of protection. How foolish we are not to spend more time within its pages.

Meditation. When we hear the word *meditation*, we often think of Eastern religions and the repetition of strange words. However, meditation is simply reflection or serious contemplation. For a Christian, it simply means focusing our attention on God. Just as prayer is simply talking to God and Bible reading is allowing God to talk to us, meditation is focusing on being aware of God and His presence.

Meditation does not necessarily require long periods of time. You can meditate for just a few minutes. But you must be alone and undisturbed, perhaps on a walk or sitting in your favorite chair while the children are still in school. You also need to choose a subject on which you wish to focus. You may choose patience or forgiveness or a particular Bible verse. Focus your thoughts and attention on this subject. Joshua instructed the people to meditate on the "Book" (Josh. 1:8). Psalm 1 tells us that the blessed or happy man meditates on the law of the Lord. David and Asaph meditated on the works of the Lord (Ps. 77:12; Ps. 143:5).

You may wish to focus your attention upon a certain relationship or problem. A few months ago I had a problem that was just too big for me. I kept pushing it aside, pretending it did not exist because I had no time to think about it and little wisdom for dealing with it. Finally, I sat down in the sun and prayed, "Let the meditation of my heart be acceptable in thy sight, O Lord." Then I focused all my attention on this problem. I thought of all that Scripture had to say pertaining to this problem; I thought of how Jesus might handle this situation. I was quiet before God, so that the Holy Spirit might reveal to me the wisdom of God (1 Cor. 2:9–10). In prayer, we speak; in meditation, we listen. I listened to the "still small voice" of God. My problem did not go away. But as I meditated I gained new assurance that God would guide me and provide strength and wisdom as I needed it. I also began to look at my problem from His point of view and had an overwhelming desire to deal with it in His way. I soon found myself focusing less on the problem and more on the power of God.

Solitude. In prayer, we talk and commune; in meditation, we listen. In solitude, we just are.

A friend of mine describes solitude as "removing the distractions." For many of us this will be difficult if not virtually impossible. But again, we are not necessarily talking about long periods of time. "Jesus Breaks" are a kind of "solitude."

Anne Morrow Lindbergh found her inner spring, her inner self, nourished through solitude and took specific times to isolate herself in order to rediscover herself. She said, "If it is a woman's function to give, she must be replenished, too."[2] I have found these times necessary not so much in order to rediscover myself as to rediscover the Lord, my best friend, and let Him replenish my parched soul. In solitude we allow God to love us, fill us, comfort us, strengthen us. We place ourselves in His eternal presence. We become very conscious of it and drink deeply from it.

Jesus Himself sought solitude in the desert, in the hills, or in a garden—any natural environment where He could best profit from solitude. Usually He went off at night or early in the morning when activity was at a minimum and noise was muted.

Someone once said so well, "The treasures of the Christian life are found in listening not speaking, in stillness rather than activity, and in the presence of God not man."

Sometimes when I was a young girl, alone in my room at night with the lights out, I would put out my hand and ask God to hold it. I felt so close to Him, so much in His presence, that I could almost feel His clasp.

This is solitude.

Fasting. For many of us, fasting is foreign. We don't know exactly what it is or if it is right for us to practice it. Yet, fasting is taught in Scripture by example. Moses fasted, as did David, Daniel, and the Lord Jesus. Fasting was observed in Scripture on occasions of public calamities, afflictions, bereavement, and approaching danger. It was usually accompanied by prayer, humiliation, and confession of sin.

Fasting is the practice of abstaining from food, eating sparingly, or denying oneself certain foods. I have some friends who feel God leading them to fast for two or three weeks at a time and other friends who fast regularly each week.

I have fasted on several occasions, as God led me, and it has been a very meaningful experience. I usually practice this particular spiritual discipline when I am at my wits' end. Like Ezra, I proclaim a fast to seek God, a right way for myself and for my little ones and for all our substance (see Ezra 8:21). For me, fasting heightens my awareness of my personal relationship with God. Each time I feel the need for food, I am aware of His presence and that my dependence is on Him and Him alone. In this state of dependency, my spiritual senses are sharpened and intensified and I am better able to hear the still small voice of the Holy Spirit directing and leading me.

ANTIDOTE FOR DRYNESS

My mother talks about a time of spiritual dryness in her life. When I was fourteen, the entire Graham family went to spend the summer in Europe. This was great fun for us but much work for Mother. Being a typical man, Daddy could not understand why packing five children for a summer in Europe was such a chore. He told mother just to place a suitcase in each child's room and tell them to fill it. She tells us of her experience in her book *It's My Turn Now*:

> Only a mother who has tried to pack for herself plus five children for several months in a foreign country will know the diffi-

> culty of this job. Finally, preparations were finished and we departed. After a long and tiring day, the plane landed in Geneva. I was too tired that night to notice much. The next morning when I awoke and pulled up the rolling blinds, I found myself looking out over Lake Geneva and the snowcapped mountains beyond. Everything was utterly charming and peaceful. That is until the children woke. Keeping house in Europe, I found, is considerably different from keeping house in America. Soon I found a good part of my time was taken up in simply keeping the family fed and the house run. The result? Spiritual drought. . . .
>
> For me, spiritual dryness usually follows an extremely busy period. Air must be still for dew to fall.
>
> One day, some friends came and took all of the children off for the day. I grabbed my Bible, found an empty chaise lounge on the portico, and there in the sun I read Job all day. I felt like the prophet fed by angels in the desert when he had reached the end of himself—fed and refreshed. When the car pulled up in the drive late that afternoon, supper was ready and I was refreshed and eager to have the children back.[3]

Mother also described her spiritual dryness in this poem:

Drifting . . . slipping . . . slow I *went;*
No *leap in sudden haste,*
but quietly I *eased away*
into this silent waste.

How long it's been, I *do not know;*
a minute from Him *seems*
like long midnights of emptiness
and silent screams.

I *heard the distant promises*
with wistfulness and groped to see
a glimmer of Him *in the dark:*
Could He *see me?*

There was no pounding on the gates,
—no cry at Heaven's *door—*

I had no strength; my tears left
A puddle on the floor.

Then from my crumpled nothingness,
My dungeon of despair,
A quiet opening of the door
—a breath of Living air.

He let me sleep, as if I'd died,
Yet when morning broke
The Risen Sun discovered me,
And I awoke.

New, I awoke; His warming love,
Updrawing, transformed everything.
Tell me—is this how an acorn falls
In Spring?[4]

Just as day always follows night, renewal will follow periods of dryness if we seek our rest and refreshment in the Lord. Remember, rest is not a luxury, it is a necessity. Inner rest and refreshment is vital in order to maintain priorities and balance in our changing world.

The answer to your problem of rest could be practical, physical, or spiritual. Take inventory and discover where you can find the time to enter into your personal retreat center and take a much-needed "vacation."

Chapter 1

1. "Women and Children Adrift," *Reader's Digest*, Sept. 1986, 91.
2. From "After the Sexual Revolution," ABC, July 30, 1986, and the *Sun Sentinel*, June 26, 1986.
3. "Too Late for Prince Charming," *Newsweek*, June 2, 1986, 54.
4. Susan Wooley and O. Wayne Wooley, "Thinness Mania," *American Health*, Oct. 1986, 68–74.
5. Elisabeth Elliott, *Let Me Be a Woman* (Wheaton: Tyndale, 1977), 54.

Chapter 2

1. Betty Friedan, *The Second Stage*, (New York: Simon and Schuster, 1982), 15–16.
2. Dee Jepsen, *Women: Beyond Equal Rights* (Waco, TX: Word, 1984), 71.
3. Anne Morrow Lindbergh, *Gift from the Sea*, (New York: Random House, 1978), 51–52.
4. Elliott, 24.
5. Ibid., 51–52, 54.
6. Edith Deen, *All of the Women of the Bible* (New York: Harper and Row, 1955), 141–142.
7. Ibid., 385.
8. George Sweeting, "D. L. Moody's Balance Wheel," *Moody Monthly*, April 1986.

Chapter 3

1. Amy Carmichael, *If* (Waco, TX: Word, 1980).

Chapter 4

1. Gordon MacDonald, *Ordering Your Private World* (Nashville: Oliver-Nelson, 1985), 12, 19.
2. Jepsen, 71.
3. Lindbergh, 80.

Chapter 5

1. More on this subject can be found in Paul Tournier's *The Gift of Feeling* (Atlanta: John Knox).
2. Jepsen, 32.
3. "Three's a Crowd," *Newsweek*, Sept. 1, 1986, 68.
4. Jepsen, 121.
5. Adapted from an article by Hilary Cosell in *The Ladies' Home Journal*, April 1985.
6. "The Mail," *Newsweek*, April 21, 1986.
7. Taken from an article by Maggie Scarf, *People*, Sept. 1980.
8. Edith Schaeffer, *Common Sense Christian Living* (Nashville: Thomas Nelson, 1983), 101.

Chapter 6

1. Candi Long, "First Person," *Moody Monthly*, May 1986, 104.

Chapter 7

1. Judith Viorst, *Alexander and the Terrible, Horrible, No Good, Very Bad Day* (New York: Atheneum, 1972).
2. Gigi Graham Tchividjian, *Thank You, Lord, for My Home* (Minneapolis: Worldwide Publications, 1980).
3. David Augsburger, *Caring Enough to Confront* (Ventura, CA: Regal, 1980), 10–11.
4. Susan Stevenson, "Mental Junk Food," *Moody Monthly*, Nov. 1984.

Chapter 8

1. Carmichael.

Chapter 10

1. MacDonald, 171. More on this subject can be found in *The Earth is the Lord's* and *Sabbath* by Abraham Heschel (New York: Farrar, Strauss, and Giroux, 1978 and 1975).
2. Lindbergh, 48.
3. Ruth Bell Graham, *It's My Turn Now* (Old Tappan, NJ: Revell, 1972).
4. Ibid.